ALAS POOR JOHNNY

ALAS POOR JOHNNY

A MEMOIR OF LIFE ON AN EXMOOR FARM

Buster Johnson

with a foreword by Boris Johnson

Edited by Birdie Johnson

MATADOR

Matador
9 Priory Business Park
Wistow Road
Kibworth Beauchamp
Leicester LE8 0RX, UK
Tel: (+44) 116 279 2299
Fax: (+44) 116 279 2277
Email: books@troubador.co.uk
Web: www.troubador.co.uk/matador

ISBN 978 1784621 827

British Library Cataloguing in Publication Data.
A catalogue record for this book is available from the British Library.

Typeset by Troubador Publishing Ltd, Leicester, UK
Printed and bound in the UK by TJ International, Padstow, Cornwall

Matador is an imprint of Troubador Publishing Ltd

For Buster and Johnny's grandchildren and great-grandchildren, and all who come after.

Birdie (ed)

Contents

Foreword

I can see it so clearly in my mind's eye – the moment my grandmother is overwhelmed by disaster.

We are in the kitchen of West Nethercote, a 14th century farmhouse on Exmoor, and though it is getting on for suppertime the sun is shining through the window behind her, illuminating her grey-fair hair and glowing through the great glass hemisphere in her hands. It is a special evening, because Granny has made her signature dish.

She is about to serve her *meisterwerk*, a main course that is to be greeted with acclaim and eaten with ravenous appetite. She is beaming, as well she may.

Many are the culinary difficulties that she has overcome.

I am not sure that she was ever really taught to cook. She was born in the Pavillon du Barry at Versailles; she went to Cheltenham Ladies College; she read Russian and got a half-blue for judo at Oxford. No, I don't think cooking featured much on her early curriculum.

It would be fair to say that her kitchen – a converted cow-byre – was not exactly a chef's paradise. She had no mixing machines. When Granny Butter (as we grandchildren used to call her) churned butter, she churned it by hand.

When the concrete floor needed cleaning, Granny would get handfuls of wet tea leaves, hurl them into the dusty corners, and sweep up the gloop with a broom.

Her fridge was a tiny cube that ran on calor gas, so frosted with surplus ice that the door would barely shut. Her stove was the Rayburn, which could take half a day to get warm, and whose lower oven was home, in the spring, to tiny orphaned lambs.

She had no collection of fancy saucepans, no Sabatier knives – and yet she produced dishes whose tastes and smells I can remember today, almost half a century later, with Proust-like rapture.

There was Granny's apple crumble, made with huge sour green apples and lemons; and in the afternoons we were invited to use her special spatula, called 'bluey', to mix the flour and the sugar and the butter together to the point where we were allowed to abandon bluey and dive our fingers in, rolling and sieving until we had thousands of buttery nodules that we knew would go golden and crunchy on top.

If there was one pudding more exciting than Granny's apple crumble, it was 'Granny's ice cream' – made by mixing Carnation milk with cocoa and pouring it into the ice trays of her fridge.

But her all-time number one creation was something she called 'risotto'. Here is the recipe for Granny Butter's risotto.

1. Boil up a large quantity of Uncle Ben's rice. 2. Chop up a load of tomatoes and onions. 3. Open several cans of tuna fish. 4. Shove them all together in the biggest bowl you can find.

Put like that it sounds a bit primitive, but it makes me hungry just to think about it. In fact the only trouble with Granny Butter's risotto was that there was never enough of it. We would lick clean the bowl in about five minutes.

Now, though, she has made a huge amount – enough to feed umpteen children, grandchildren and other hangers-on. She holds high the heavenly half-orb, smiling a smile of triumph. And as she does so the heavy bowl slips squeaking through her damp fingers.

It falls from her hands. It strikes a glancing blow on the white enamel-topped table and then shatters into a million fragments on the floor.

There is a silence. We look in horror at the waste and desolation, the glass shards winking in the tuna. Someone starts to cry.

What does Granny do?

'Never mind,' she cries, waving her arm theatrically, imperiously. 'I am sure it will be delicious!'

And by God she scoops up the entire mess, and puts it in another bowl and then serves it up, and leads by eating it herself, her bright eyes daring us to do the same. So we follow her example. And of course it IS delicious, if a bit crunchy now and then.

Granny Butter's key quality was her unconquerable optimism.

Nethercote is the farm high in the Exe valley where she and my grandfather had lived since 1952. It is a place of wild and romantic beauty – just about the most remote and unspoiled valley I can think of in England. But there can be days when it demands a bit of mental fortitude.

Granny had no dishwasher and no washing machine and no central heating, and she had electricity supplied by a diesel generator that was constantly packing up.

She had to cope with my grandfather and four children and everyone who was trying to help him make a living out of this spectacular but unprofitable piece of semi-moor. At one stage she had to cope with 13 dogs, not all of them perfectly house-trained.

There was Kylie, the big red and white sheepdog, who bit me – quite properly – when I tried to ride him like a horse. There was Shebie and Coca and Cola and Crumpy and Scrumpy and Janey and Rogue, and above all there was an especially aggressive and territorial terrier called Tiddles, my grandfather's favourite.

They filled the house with their irrefutable doggy presence – but no crime they committed, no mess they made, nothing they did could damage the dogs in the esteem of Granny Butter. Dogs were amazingly intelligent and loyal, she would explain – even though her own repeatedly ate her hearing aid, or chewed it beyond repair. And so, in her view, were most members of the animal kingdom.

She even loved the geese. These were by some way the most frightening animals on the farm. They would come charging towards you with necks arched, orange tongues vibrating in their gaping beaks.

'Don't run, darling,' Granny would say. 'They can sense your fear. All animals can sense your fear.'

Granny didn't run from the geese, or tiptoe past them. She would stride towards them, chanting her special feeding-time song, 'Foodee, foodee, foodee-foodee FoodEEE,' and out of her bucket she would hurl a wide arc of grain through the air.

The geese would honk with pleasure and truffle for the golden nuggets in the grass. They liked Granny; Granny liked them.

The animals were often ill, with 'blackleg' and other appalling-sounding complaints. But if they were ill, it was just the way things were, a function of the general harshness of the environment. It wasn't through lack of care from Granny.

She would take orphan lambs, and feed them by hand, and she would let us grandchildren help her. I remember the gulping speed with which they would drain the big bottles of powdered milk, their little throats rising and falling as they glugged it down.

Not unreasonably, the lambs often formed the impression that Granny was their mother. Everywhere that Granny went, they were sure to go – and so would we.

Granny had that essential requirement of charm: she always looked genuinely pleased to see you.

'Hello, darling!' she would cry, and she would immediately come up with some project for entertainment or education. She took us down to a little dam we had made in the Exe, where she taught us to swim, touching the slippery brown stones with the tips of our fingers and keeping our noses just above water as we thrashed our feet.

She taught us to skim stones, and afterwards, on the sunny bank, she taught us to read.

She encouraged us to climb as high as we could in the trees. When the weather was really foul we would play Ludo or Scrabble or Beggar My Neighbour or bagatelle, with wooden spoons as the cues.

If we were very lucky indeed, we were allowed to play her own special game – the ultimate form of indoor entertainment.

It is called Granny Butter's Sofa Game. Such is my nostalgia that I have often wondered whether I could get someone to commission the format for a TV game show.

One team goes out of the room and the other busies itself with a great pile of cushions and blankets under which a number of them conceal themselves on the old green sofa. The first team has to guess how many people there are hiding there. The second team has to fool them, for instance with strategically placed shoes and gloves.

Believe me, it takes character to lie rigid under those cushions, as people poke and tease you. As games go, it is a terrific ice-breaker, and Granny was wonderful at pretending to be surprised at whoever was in the sofa.

But I don't want to suggest that she spoiled us. She also imposed discipline.

She led us in the chores necessary for survival at Nethercote. We had to get the wood fire going in the middle kitchen (as the sitting room was known). We had to fill and light the paraffin 'Aladdin' stoves; and then, since none of these produced much heat, we battled to keep shut all the ill-fitting doors.

The drafts were so bad that Granny gave you half a chocolate Smartie if you were seen shutting a door; and took a whole Smartie back if she caught you leaving one open.

She insisted on good manners. Children were expected to get up when adults – and especially ladies – came into the room. Crisps – bafflingly – had to be eaten with a knife and fork.

I am afraid that this caused us uncontrollable laughter, as did her occasional pretensions to have noble ancestors called the 'de Pfeffels'.

'All the crowned heads of Europe,' she once said, while we giggled helplessly at the idea. It was only much later in life that I found she was entirely right. She was descended from kings – if on the wrong side of the blanket.

As for her own legacy, it bobs up irresistibly down the generations. We are now on the fourth generation of Granny Butter's progeny, and there are traces of her everywhere: she is there in the beaky noses, the fair hair, the sturdy proportions.

More importantly, I would say she was the ancestor and perhaps the progenitor of that spirit of optimism and exuberance that some of them exhibit – from time to time – to this day.

It is wonderful to hear her voice again, and remember how she played the sunbeam of her kindness on all the people and animals of Nethercote valley.

Boris Johnson

Preface

My mother Irène (known as Buster) was 29 when she married Johnny, in 1936, swapping her cultured upper middle class life for one of frequent chaos and uncertainty. From wartime wife (via Surrey smallholding) to isolated Exmoor farm, she took it in her stride, immersing herself in her new life as if she had known no other. Her world shrank, revolving around her husband and their four children – my two brothers, my sister and myself.

Voluble and vivacious, in spite of increasing deafness, she was the antithesis of our father, who was not a man to use two words where one – or none – would do. But she adored him. 'I love that man,' she would say, catching sight of him crossing the yard.

As we children went away to school, grew older and scattered about the country (and later the world) we would write a weekly letter home, although we were indifferent correspondents between ourselves. But we had no need to worry about losing touch with our siblings, for my mother typed out all our letters in triplicate, sending copies to the rest of us with her own newsy epistle. We returned her letters to her, when we remembered. They joined the growing pile in one of her many cardboard boxes, stored against the day when she would write a book about her life on an Exmoor farm.

Thus it was that when, in the winter of 1960/61, her sister Denise invited her on a painting holiday to the West Indies, she leapt at the opportunity. In the hold of their cargo boat, along with my aunt's painting paraphernalia, went a portable typewriter and a large quantity of paper and carbon paper. My mother was going to write her book. She was 53.

In the West Indies, the sisters fell into a daily routine, rising at 6.00am to drive up into the hills. While Den painted in the early morning light, my mother sat on a camping chair, typewriter perched on her knee and a bag of old letters at her feet to jog her memory. At 9.00am they would return to their guest house for breakfast, then go to a nearby beach for a swim. After lunch and a siesta, my aunt switched to her afternoon painting while my mother settled herself with the typewriter on a shady verandah.

In the evening, at dinner, she would read the day's instalment to her appreciative sister. Perhaps as they talked over their meal she elaborated on her life, nudged into expansiveness by the day's burst of creativity and a clarity of vision achievable only through distance.

For four months this became more or less the pattern of their days as they moved about the islands, with breaks for sight-seeing and social life. By the time they packed their bags to return, my aunt had completed some 16 canvases and my mother the first draft of her book. With her usual generosity of spirit – for it isn't immediately apparent he is the long-suffering husband she thought she was portraying – she called it *Alas Poor Johnny*.

Back at home, the demands of farm and family all too soon absorbed her and in due course the book became abandoned. It sat on top of the medicine cupboard in the bathroom, waiting for my father to have time to read it. Years later, when they retired and moved from West Nethercote, the main farmhouse, to Nethercote Cottage, the book went too, shut away in a drawer of her desk. Eventually she died, then my father died, and the book stayed in the desk in its orange folder. Until one day I took it out, undid the string with which she had tied it up, and started reading.

This is it.

Birdie Johnson

CHAPTER 1

Early Days

Few people can have been less qualified than I was to become a farmer's wife. Town bred, and reared in the luxury of a comfortable, well-staffed middle class home, I had been groomed by my French mother for the diplomatic arena.

My father was English, had been educated at Harrow and Oxford, and was an underwriter at Lloyds. He was the eldest grandson of George Williams, who founded the Young Men's Christian Association. George Williams was born on a Somerset farm near Dulverton, on the southern edge of Exmoor, the eighth son of a sheep farmer. He overturned a load of hay when he was a boy and his father told him he would never make a farmer, so he went to London and joined a firm of wholesale drapers.

George was a devout Christian and the YMCA, founded by him with 12 members from among his fellow apprentices, soon spread throughout the world. He married the daughter of the head of the firm, taking over from him when he retired. He was knighted by Queen Victoria, given the Freedom of the City of London and buried in the crypt of St Paul's Cathedral.

Occasionally George visited his farming family in Somerset, although I believe few of his children ever went there. His eldest son was my grandfather, for whom the humble farm of his forebears was already left far behind in the mists of Exmoor.

Snobbery was creeping in. My grandfather sent his three sons to Harrow and warned them that if they were asked by their schoolfellows what their father (whom they called '*pater*') did, they should reply that he was a professional man, since it wasn't considered quite the thing to be 'in trade'.

My father became a member of Lloyds when he came down from Oxford. We lived in a large, comfortable house in Bromley, Kent, and my closest connection with a farm, until I was 17, was fetching the milk from Mrs Wearn's during Cornish holidays at Carbis Bay.

My mother's father, Baron Jean Marie François Christian Frederick Hubert de Pfeffel, was the last of a long line of de Pfeffels first officially mentioned in the 13th century, when one of them was a troubadour. They were of Alsatian stock, and as Alsace sometimes changed hands between France and Germany, so they changed nationality. They were French in 1907 when I was born, in my grandfather's home in Versailles.

This was a magnificent house in the Avenue de Paris called *le Pavillon du Barry*, which had once belonged to Madame du Barry, mistress of Louis XV. It was elegantly furnished and well-staffed and my childhood memories are of vast inter-communicating reception rooms with gleaming parquet flooring and crystal chandeliers, tapestries and damasks, with footmen flitting quietly in and out and Athanase, the *maître d'hotel*, announcing '*Madame la Baronne est servie.*' My sister Den and I were taken there from England every summer until the Great War. After the war, my grandfather died and the beautiful house was sold.

By this time, I had three sisters: Den, two years younger, and Niki and Minki, twins, who had been born in 1916. We all spoke French and English indiscriminately, and still do, using among ourselves whichever language springs first to mind. Our beloved English nanny was replaced by a French governess. She was succeeded, for the two eldest of us, by a penniless Russian princess who had fled the Russian revolution with only the clothes she was wearing. These were getting pretty threadbare by the time she reached us and the poor princess Olga was certainly quite incapable of teaching us to darn and mend, for she had never learnt. She wore one pair of stockings over another in the futile hope that the holes wouldn't coincide.

But we never needed to learn this menial task. We were brought up shockingly, with maids to do our mending and tidy away our clothes, and it wasn't until Den and I arrived at Cheltenham Ladies' College, two French speaking little 'Froggies' aged 13 and 11, that we were faced with the appalling conundrum of having to darn our black wool stockings.

At school, my French name, Irène, was a stumbling block to many people and the cause of some embarrassment to me, for the best my Latin mistress could manage was 'Urine, dear.' I later acquired the nickname 'Buster', which made life simpler.

Our parents had a large cosmopolitan circle of friends; intelligent, musical, artistic, well-read and well-informed, with lively minds. They often gave dinner parties and our home was open to all and sundry every Sunday. Conversation flowed at mealtimes. When eventually my husband Johnny, one of those quiet men who is inclined to measure his words, was thrust into this monkey house, he never got a word in edgeways. He has often told me that he should have seen the red light then. Poor Johnny. Watching him anxiously, I could see his mouth opening from time to time and then closing again philosophically. In the end he never even attempted to open his lips – and he speaks with them closed to this day, so that I am continually mishearing what he says and getting into trouble.

My mother was musical, and several well-known pianists have played on our Bechstein Grand and famous singers have graced our Bromley drawing-room. Meanwhile my father retired downstairs to the billiard room with his cronies (Johnny among them), where they couldn't hear the thumping and warbling. My sisters and I were nurtured on Beethoven, Schubert, Chopin and Fauré.

Six years at Cheltenham were followed by three years at Oxford, where I read French, with Russian as a special subject. I never took Russian in my Finals because half-way through the course my professor committed suicide.

During school holidays and university vacations my sisters and I continued our education in the broader sense. We were taken abroad every summer until we had visited most European countries and had also been to North and South Africa. We paid frequent visits to Paris, where our French grandmother and aunt lived, and where we were escorted round the museums, art galleries and monuments of interest, but did not, I am afraid, show any marked enthusiasm.

At home we went to concerts, to London theatres, to Covent Garden, the Russian Ballet, Nikita Ballieff's *Chauve Souris*; also to Wimbledon, to the Chelsea Flower Show and, with our father, to the Varsity rugger match every year and to public school matches. He was a great enthusiast. We were fitted for the leisurely, comfortable life of upper middle class girls of those days and my mother had secret hopes that I would marry an Ambassador, because of my languages.

We never learnt to cook. In fact we seldom entered the kitchen; the cook came to my mother daily for orders. It wasn't until I reached Oxford that I learnt to make cocoa and scrambled eggs in the little pantry outside our bedsitters.

After I came down from Oxford I spent six months idling at home; reading, helping my mother arrange the flowers, going with her on shopping sprees to London in her chauffeur-driven Daimler and accompanying her to the bridge club. Both my parents were excellent players and I started to learn bridge before I was nine. I became reasonably competent and enjoyed the game immensely and it is a real privation for me never to play now. Most other things from my past I haven't minded giving up at all, but I do miss the bridge.

While at home I took a secretarial training course and had various secretarial jobs in London. Then my parents, whose solution for getting me out of what they considered to be unsuitable romantic entanglements was to take me or send me abroad, had me dispatched to Cairo, where a friend of mine was working. The opportunity was more than I could resist; despite twanging heartstrings, I sailed without delay.

It was in Egypt that I met Johnny, who was managing an estate there.

Johnny was two years younger than me and had spent most of his time since leaving school working on farms, both in England and in Canada. His father was Turkish, but he had been brought up in Bournemouth by his English grandmother,

5

his mother having died of puerperal fever a few weeks after he was born. His father, Ali Kemal, was a writer and publisher, with a passionate interest in the politics of his country. These beliefs frequently made him unpopular, and in 1922, on the verge of leaving Istanbul for England, he was kidnapped by agents of the government and murdered. Johnny has no memory of either parent. As a boy, he had wanted to fly but had not been allowed to. Farming was his second choice.

In 1935, after three years in Egypt, I returned to England. Johnny followed. With no farming prospects in view, he was offered and accepted a job in a timber brokers' office in London. A year later we were married.

CHAPTER 2

Braunton and Parley Brook

Johnny did his job to the best of his ability, but he loathed city life. We lived in Kent, at Keston, and drove out into the country at weekends in his old Lancia Lamda, which he had brought home from Egypt, but he always felt he was suffocating the moment he stepped out of the train at Cannon Street in the mornings.

At home, my new home, I had an excellent Bavarian cook-general and my mother insisted on providing me with a Bavarian nanny for my first born. I would be tied, she said, if I had to wash nappies and sterilise feeding bottles. Johnny disagreed, but he was overruled and I was still too much *la demoiselle de la maison* to have a proper sense of values.

I continued to play bridge with my mother in the afternoons and accompany her on her jaunts; I gave little tea parties for my friends and invited them to dinner, using our new silver and cut glass and table linen – all polished and crisply ironed for me. The household ran on oiled wheels and it mattered not at all that I had no idea how to wash woollies or clean a lavatory pan, nor what detergent to use, nor the difference between plain and self-raising flour. I arranged the flowers, had long telephone conversations and produced another baby.

Then my bliss was shattered overnight.

My two Bavarians, in 1939, were ordered by their Embassy to return to Germany, under threat of never seeing their families again if they stayed. Simultaneously, my mother lost her entire staff. Chaos reigned. Their departure marked the end of an era; my long apprenticeship had begun.

Johnny was domesticated, in a manner of speaking, for he had made shift for himself in Canada, and he taught me to cook; when he got home from the city in the evening he wielded the frying pan while I watched. He also taught me to iron.

I got a Mrs Dunn to come in daily 'to oblige'. All I can remember about her is that she had had a 15lb baby and thought she held the record. My second son weighed 10lbs (all but 3oz to be truthful) and whenever I have boasted to other proud mothers with eight and nine pounders I have guiltily remembered Mrs Dunn.

As soon as war seemed imminent, Johnny joined the Civil Air Guard and learnt to fly. At last he had achieved the great wish of his boyhood. The war years were marvellous years for him. He was a pilot in Coastal Command, on anti-U boat patrol, and was awarded the DFC for his skill and coolness in emergencies. He got very badly smashed up and burnt towards the end of the war and was in and out of hospital for over a year. He couldn't wait to fly again, although he was told he never would, and eventually went back to it.

When the war ended he wasn't demobilised until 1947 as he was still under medical supervision. There had been some question of breaking his leg again to reset it, though in the end it wasn't done and one leg is permanently two inches shorter than the other.

By then we had four children; Peter, Hilary, Stanley and Gillian (whom we nicknamed Birdie), aged nine, eight, seven and two. I had spent the greater part of the war living with the children at my parents' home in Cornwall, where they had moved to escape the Bromley blitz, though my mother, sadly, died shortly before Gillian was born. With my menagerie it was impossible to find digs near Johnny, who was shifted about, and in any case strongly disapproved of wives near operational stations.

But we did all spend three years in a cottage at Braunton, in Devon, overlooking the runway at Chivenor, from which I had a grandstand view of his final 'prang'. Gillian was born in Braunton and the two boys went to Ravenswood, a preparatory school near Tiverton.

We fell in love with North Devon and the Devon people, who were so friendly and took us to their hearts, and it was then that we first acquired our love of the West Country. The countryside was beautiful; you couldn't see the hedges for primroses and violets in the spring and there were wild strawberries to gather in the woods and mushrooms in the fields near the cottage.

They were three very happy years for me, in spite of the anxiety, for many of our friends were killed. Somehow I never thought it could happen to us. Johnny had always been so cool and so completely the master of any situation that I don't think it occurred to me that he might not pull through.

In the evenings, when he wasn't on operations, and I had a babysitter, we would go down to the New Inn at Braunton and play shove-halfpenny for our beer. I became rather expert and didn't often have to buy the beer. In those days shove-halfpenny was played in nearly all the pubs in the area. Now it has been replaced by darts almost everywhere, to my sorrow, for darts is not my game.

One night, when we were enjoying a quiet pint, a new face appeared in our midst.

Somebody identified the stranger to Johnny and later he said to me, 'You see that chap over there? Well, he farms on Exmoor. Very tough fellows they are out there, terrifically hardy. He lives on an isolated farm on the moor and has ridden all the way in on his pony on a night like this.'

I gazed at this fellow from Mars with awe. I was tremendously impressed and can see him now, sitting in a corner with his cloth cap and breeches and leather gaiters and smelling of warm pony. I knew nothing about Exmoor. It sounded like the back of beyond, as indeed it was, and I thought, in French as I often do, '*Très peu pour moi.*' Not up my street! I still thought in terms of streets then, not yet of roads and lanes and sheep tracks and bridleways.

When Johnny was finally demobilised he returned to his city firm and the daily commuting to London began again – and with it the feeling that he couldn't breathe in that fume-poisoned air. He had escaped for eight years of flying and freedom and now he was back where he had started; worse than where he started, for colleagues who had been his juniors were now in positions senior to him.

We bought a house in Surrey, called *Parley Brook House*, at Horsell, near Woking. It had three acres of land, including a paddock with a stable. It seemed princely to me. We had never owned a paddock, let alone a stable, and I was thrilled.

Soon, to my delight, we had a horse in the paddock, for a

Gypsy asked if he could graze his big piebald there. There was a summer-house which turned round and a greenhouse with a vine in it and a harness room. It felt grand to own all these exotic delights. To crown it all, Horsell Common was just a few minutes away and I could make free of it with Leader and Minky, our two Labradors.

My cup of joy overflowed; London was only half an hour away by train, but I had now become a countrywoman – so I thought. Johnny, of course, knew better, although he let me keep my illusions.

We bought a hen-house and some white Leghorn pullets. Then we built pigsties near the stable and bought Bessie, Rascal and Lopears, three Large White gilts. All three were already in pig, expecting their first litters.

We knew nothing about pigs when we started, but our gardener, Arthur, had once been a cowman and was very knowledgeable about animals. He was an excellent fellow. He came to my rescue on a number of occasions when Johnny was away and I had to deal with an unexpectedly farrowing pig, or sick hen.

As we became more established, our pigs proved a profitable sideline. Johnny arranged with the restaurants and hospitals in Woking to collect pig swill from them, leaving the empty bins on his way to the station in the morning and picking them up again in the evening, filled with kitchen waste. He was a familiar figure driving the open Lancia in his city suit with two or three large dustbins piled on the back seat.

Three years went by. Then one evening Johnny came home from the office and announced that he had that morning handed in his resignation. I received the news with relief rather than alarm, for I knew how frustrated he had been feeling.

We increased our output of eggs and pigs. There was a ready market, since rationing hadn't ended with the war. The swill round was greatly extended and Johnny collected refuse from the Army camp some miles away. It was all boiled in a huge cast iron boiler in the paddock and the children's job and mine was to keep the fire going underneath it with a constant supply of logs until this witches' brew was bubble-bubbling.

We carried on in this way for a year and did quite well, except we found the profit was insufficient to meet the ever-growing family expenses. We needed more land in order to expand the business.

Through one of our friends in the West Country we heard of a hill sheep farm which might suit us and Johnny rode down on his motorcycle to have a look. That night he got chatting to some young locals in a pub at Bampton, not far from Dulverton. One of them had been rabbiting a few days earlier at a farm called West Nethercote, near Winsford, and heard that it was for sale. The place was so remote and inaccessible he couldn't imagine anyone ever wanting to live there. Thinking to play a joke on Johnny, he recommended he go and see it.

Less than 24 hours later, Johnny was back at the pub, buying him a drink in thanks. He had liked the place so much he and the farmer had shaken hands on it on the spot. He was going back the following day to clinch the deal. The next thing that happened was that I received a letter from him saying he had made an offer, which had been accepted.

So the farm was ours, subject to contract. In this matter-of-fact way I came into my Elysean fields, so different from my mother's Champs Elysées in Paris, and our children into their heritage.

CHAPTER 3

The Move

Johnny told me later that as soon as he set eyes on the farm he knew this was what we had been waiting for. In fact he knew long before he had his first glimpse of it. Riding his motorcycle up the rough track running along the river Exe, through a lovely secluded valley which seemed to belong to another world, he said to himself, 'This is it. If there's a farm up here, this is where I want to live.'

It was his idea of heaven. The more remote his surroundings, the more untouched by civilisation, the happier he is.

West Nethercote is a hill farm in the heart of Exmoor. The Exe, flowing from Exford to Winsford, runs below the house, from which it is separated by a meadow called the Splat. The river is still in its infancy, not many miles from its source as it meanders through our valley. The water is clear and sparkling and you can see trout darting upstream. But after heavy or continuous rain it can turn into a menacing surge of racing brown water, carrying great branches and sometimes drowned animals in its headlong rush.

The house is 760ft above sea level and our land rises up behind it, facing southwards. The top fields are some 1300ft above the sea. From the top of the farm, 'up over' as they say here, we look north towards the Bristol Channel. Between us and the coast lie the moor and Dunkery Beacon, the highest point on Exmoor. To the east are the Brendon hills. To the south and west, the moor spreads its purple folds in summer, when the hills are cloaked with heather and gorse and whortleberries; in winter it stretches naked to the horizon, grand in its immensity and desolation.

The Nethercote valley forms part of the Exe valley, a sheltered oasis in the rugged isolation of the moor. Because of the height, our soil can't compare with that of the lowland pastures and it offers no easy livelihood. Johnny has to work hard to make a living and it was years before he took his first holiday.

The farmhouse itself has enormous character. This was just an extra bonus for us. As far as Johnny was concerned, it was the land that counted; the house was unimportant and he knew I would agree. As it turned out, I would never want a different house. I loved it, and everything about the farm, from the moment I saw it. We have lived here ten years now and I never want to live anywhere else.

When we go down to the local for the odd pint I listen to farming talk: what are the latest market prices, where was the pack laid on during the previous day's hunt, where to buy a ram or sell a Landrover or find someone free to do some hedging or help with the shearing. This is the conversation to which I have now become accustomed and the other kind, my old kind, has almost completely vanished with the dreaming spires and the London fogs. Our life in Surrey, which had seemed to me so ideal, was just an interval while waiting for the real thing.

I enjoy going away from time to time. I love my visits to London, where I see my sisters and my old friends. But my new roots, grown so late in life (for I was 44 when we came to Nethercote) have reached down deep into the Somerset soil. So, too, have the children's; for they have all grown up here and I know that whatever the future holds for them, wherever they may be, they will look upon the farm as their home.

Indeed, it is probable that our roots reach back further than ten years. For not only do we now find ourselves just ten miles from Dulverton, where my great-grandfather, George Williams, was born, but the parish records reveal that in 1770 one of his ancestors, Robert Williams, actually married in Winsford. Through some strange coincidence I have returned to the land of my forefathers, those generations of Somerset farmers with whom I thought I had so little in common. I only have to sit in the firelight by the huge open hearth of an evening or to watch the sun setting over the hills, turning pink the autumn bracken, while a heron drifts over the river or a fox barks across the valley, to know that this is where I belong.

However, lest I should sound too starry-eyed, I must add that I don't always have this feeling of destiny. At times in winter, when our supply of hedge trimmings for the fire is lying buried in a snowdrift and the east wind is driving the smoke back down our so picturesque old chimneys – at such times, when the dogs are barking, the phone ringing and I have just burnt my wrist on the oven tray – then I feel that I belong almost anywhere else on earth.

When we took over West Nethercote our only immediate neighbours were Mrs Stevens and her son Victor, at East Nethercote, a short distance away. The only other house,

Nethercote Cottage, was empty, having recently changed hands. The new owners kindly agreed to let it to us unfurnished while some alterations were in progress at our house.

In the late summer of 1951, we sold Parley Brook House, together with all our pigs except Bessie. We took Bessie with us, and some of the poultry. Most of our furniture left before we did, in two pantechnicons, and was to be unloaded into the cottage ready for our arrival. We were to follow a few days later with the animals.

Thus it was that on the morning of Sunday 7 October we loaded up the animals and the cavalcade set off. Arthur, our gardener, was with us, for he had decided to throw in his lot with ours and brave the wilds of Exmoor. There were just the three of us, for the boys were away at boarding school and the girls staying in Cornwall with my father over the move. We only got as far as Chobham, two miles away, where we nipped into the White Hart for a last farewell. We were given a rousing send-off, and soon after 2.00pm emerged fortified for our journey.

To my unutterable relief Johnny, who was driving a two-ton van while I drove the Lancia, was called back indoors at the last moment and I was able to sneak off ahead and get a good start on him, so he couldn't hear me change gear.

I ought to say 'so he couldn't hear my attempts to change gear', since for the first half-hour I never managed to change down at all; when it became impossible for me to proceed in top gear, I was obliged to wave all traffic behind me to a standstill, stop dead, get into bottom and change up until I reached the gear required. This was not my fault. The Lancia, of 1927 vintage, was Johnny's most precious possession. I hadn't driven since before the war, but he had to drive the van loaded with livestock, so was faced with the dreadful necessity of putting me in charge of it. Only he and his fellow Lancia enthusiasts could change down on this particular model without making the most agonising noise. He made no secret of the fact that he didn't expect me to reach Nethercote.

For company I had Arthur and Leader, one of our two Labradors. Johnny had Minky.

Eventually I mastered the gears sufficiently to make some sort of a change down, if not exactly a smooth one, and the Lancia went like a bird; I felt as if I was a potential world champion winning the *Mille Miglia*. The only slight drawback was that every time I applied the foot brake the handbrake came on of its own accord and remained on. It took quite a bit of strength to yank it off again and Arthur and I worked out a combined operation whereby I warned him whenever I touched the foot brake and he at once wrestled with the other.

We reached Bampton by 7.00pm, as darkness was falling. Another half-hour should have seen us to Winsford, except that once clear of Bampton we plunged into the thickest blanket of fog I have ever met. Hugging the verge and leaning out to see, I passed and re-passed the same quarry and the same sawmill, now on our right and now to our left, and there was a round house which loomed out of the fog right in the centre of crossroads and up to which we crept every half-hour or so from the four points of the compass.

This nightmare finally ended when we reached Nethercote at 10.00pm, cold, stiff and tired, having sailed over two narrow wooden bridges spanning the Exe with only inches to spare. That didn't worry me as I had driven up the lane oblivious of them and only saw them the next day. The second one had no railings because the removal men had had to take them down to get their vans across. They told us later that only the inner wheels of their double wheels rested on the bridge as they crossed, the outer ones revolving in space.

It had taken the men with the vans four hours to negotiate the last two miles to our farm, almost as long as the journey from Surrey, cutting down overhanging trees as they went.

There was no sign of Johnny when Arthur, Leader and I finally arrived. Mrs Stevens, at East Nethercote, made us welcome and we toasted ourselves by her log fire, seated on the old wooden settle by the huge fireplace, while she brought us food and a warm drink. It was bliss. I felt tired but triumphant; we had made it, we had beaten Johnny to it and confounded all his prophecies of doom.

When we were rested, we made our way to the cottage; there was no electricity and I could only find an almost extinct torch in the Lancia. Chaos greeted us. The men had been unable to get most of our big furniture through the door and had left it in the garage. The rest had been dumped anywhere, at random, all piled up in a heap of mattresses, cushions, curtains and smaller items of furniture.

I went back to Mrs Stevens for a light and she lent me a candle. Between us Arthur and I dragged out mattresses, searched for bedding and cleared enough space to make up beds on the floor. By this time it was midnight and we needed a cup of tea. I found a packet of tea and some cups and a primus stove and the meths, but no kettle. So we boiled the water in one of the dogs' dishes, by the feeble light of the dying torch because the candle had burnt out. Never did a cup of tea taste better.

At 1.00am Johnny arrived, having had a particularly eventful journey. He had left Chobham with the van shortly after us, with Minky sitting beside him. The back was filled to capacity with Bessie, furniture and hens, ducks and geese, in that order, to preserve the poultry from Bessie's attentions.

In the end, it wasn't the poultry that needed preservation but Johnny himself. Bessie's compartment was immediately behind the driving seat, divided off by stout wooden crossbars; behind her was a wall of furniture keeping her from the stacked crates of poultry. They hadn't gone far before she broke down the barricade and inserted her snout under Johnny's posterior. She then gave a heave and his foot leapt off the accelerator and his head hit the roof.

He tried to pen her in again and again but she defied all his efforts. She enjoyed her little game and never tired of it, so he spent the rest of the day flying through the air at intervals. Whenever he felt her snout burrowing underneath him he had to take a hand off the wheel and grab the nearest solid support.

When they finally reached Taunton, he decided to take a short cut across the Brendon hills rather than go the longer way round via Bampton. He had barely embarked on this cross-country road when the fog clamped down on him. All he could do was lean out and try to follow the contour of the hedge. In those days there were no white markings at junctions with side roads; so he missed the right turning he should have taken and took some left forks he should have avoided. The Brendons stretch for mile after mile with hardly a habitation and very few signposts, so he just went on turning in circles in the fog.

When at last he drove safely over our second bridge and through East Nethercote yard towards West Nethercote his troubles weren't yet over, for one of his wheels became embedded in a concealed ditch at the side of the lane between the two farmhouses. He had to wake up Victor Stevens so they could tow the van out with the tractor.

By the time the livestock had been unloaded and Bessie fed and bedded down there wasn't much of the night left.

CHAPTER 4

West Nethercote

West Nethercote farmhouse is a long, low rectangular stone building, with walls four feet thick or more which have withstood the ravages of five or six centuries and are likely to be still standing in another 500 years. Originally the roof was thatched, but in the 1890s the thatch was replaced by slates and the roof raised.

Under the eaves, house martins build their nests. After rain, we watch them flitting around the puddles in the yard, scooping up beakfuls of damp earth, then darting up to weld their nests to the rough walls by means of this clay so laboriously gathered. We have swallows too, which nest in the stables year after year. Shearing takes place in there, but they fly in and out with food for their young ones, regardless of the thrumming of the diesel engine and the stir of men and sheep within a few feet of them.

Like the swallows, the builders of old had their own methods of making things stick. Our bedroom walls are made of lath and plaster, held together with cow hair and dried dung; but the thick outer walls had nothing to keep them standing throughout the centuries apart from the awe-inspiring skill of their builders, for cement was unknown and stone was piled upon stone with only packed earth to hold them in place.

Our builder brought to light massive oak beams all over the house, hewn in solid blocks from vast tree trunks which had once spread their branches over the forefathers of the first Elizabethans. Successive generations of country folk, so inured to such beauty that their eye no longer beheld it and anxious only to minimise the labour of keeping the rooms clean, had plastered over them or blocked them off, presumably to eliminate the odd nooks and crevices where dust and cobwebs collected.

I prefer to gaze at my beamed ceilings and let my mind wander back over the centuries, no matter how many spiders make their homes there. In any case, for the first few years, when our only means of lighting was with oil lamps, their gentle radiance never reached into the darker recesses; no spring-cleaning compulsion ever drove me to probe those immemorial crannies with a long handled broom.

When we arrived, the only water to the house came from a tap outside, so there was no bathroom or lavatory – just an Elsan in one of the bedrooms, screened by a plywood partition. From this bedroom, at the eastern end, you step through a low arched oak door onto the twisting stone staircase which leads down to the room below. This was known then, and is still known now, as the back kitchen.

There is another staircase in the middle of the house, which descends into the middle kitchen. The reason for these two different kitchens is that in the old days West Nethercote employed a fair number of farm hands. Some of them lived on the premises and cooked their food in the back kitchen, climbing the stone stairs at night to sleep in the loft above. The farmer and his family lived and cooked in the middle kitchen, using the other staircase to retire to their sleeping quarters.

There was a third living room, called the parlour. This room, originally at the western end of the house until an outhouse extension was added, was thought by our builder to have been the byre. He remarked that farmers of old liked to house their cattle alongside their living rooms for mutual warmth in winter.

The parlour became Johnny's office – a functional sign of the times. We transformed the adjoining outhouse into our present kitchen, linked to the rest of the house by a passage running the length of the parlour, and converted the loft above it into a bathroom, lavatory and small bedroom. The middle kitchen became our sitting-room and the back kitchen underwent many vicissitudes, being used for different purposes. We continue to call them by their original names, so we appear to have three different kitchens but no sitting-room or dining-room, which is rather confusing for visitors.

The two original kitchens are low-ceilinged rooms with thick oak beams and enormous fireplaces, inside which you can stand and peer up at the sky at the top of the chimney, and down which, in bad weather, the rain spatters onto the sizzling logs.

We no longer light the middle kitchen fire in the summer, since we have a Rayburn and a calor gas stove for cooking, although I keep it going all winter. It was Mrs Stevens who taught me how to keep the fire in without ever having to relight it, as she taught me so many other things.

At night, before going to bed, you pick up with an ancient pair of iron tongs any partly consumed logs and place them at the back of the hearth, shovelling over them a coating of hot ash until they are completely covered. They will go on smouldering gently under the ash all through the night and the following day, until such time as you require a cheerful blaze. Then all you have to do is rake the ashes forward, uncovering the glowing bits of wood, throw some fresh logs on top and use a pair of bellows. In no time the flames are dancing merrily. I have sometimes left the fire under a layer of ash for 48 hours before reviving it, without having to use paper or a match.

If the rain has been pouring down the open chimney all night and the ashes are wet it is not so rewarding. I have often knelt on the stone floor until my knees ached, working away with the bellows and muttering dark curses, with other jobs waiting to be done and visitors due at any moment. Many a time I have shamefully cheated by pouring generous libations of paraffin onto the damp wood and putting a match to it, a ruse which Johnny would never sink to. He is a wizard with fires, piling up great sections of tree trunk one on top of the other and having them crackling away in no time. I am always thankful when he volunteers for the job.

Unfortunately he suffers from a little failing common to us all; he can't see anyone else in the act of lighting a fire without informing him or her that they are going the wrong way about it and will never get it to go. Just as the perspiring performer is at last rewarded by a feeble glimmer from the smoky depths, his/her premature sigh of relief is extinguished by Johnny, whose itching fingers are longing to get at it. In a jiffy the carefully positioned logs are torn apart, the hard won flicker vanishes and he begins, with kind advice and busy confidence, to rearrange the edifice according to his own notions.

We are all the same; we can't resist it any more than we can resist reaching for a jar lid which someone else has failed to unscrew. The trouble is you never get the chance to crow over Johnny because he always succeeds with whatever he undertakes. He knows the right way to set about a job and if, for some reason beyond his control, he can't use the correct method then he will improvise another which achieves his objective. He is a master at effecting temporary repairs without the proper tools when we are stuck in the wilds; bits of wire from gate posts, silver paper to replace a burnt out fuse, scraps of metal and people's belts have all been pressed into service.

Nothing defeats him. Since nursery days the children have heard me say, 'We'll ask Daddy,' 'Daddy will do it,' and he does.

While the middle kitchen remains our sitting room, the back kitchen has undergone numerous transformations, often at a few hours' notice, completely changing its character and its appearance from one day to the next. During lambing it has been cleared of all furniture, its concrete floor strewn with straw and our solid old nursery fireguard placed in front of the fireplace. The room then becomes both hospital and nursery to motherless lambs, with outside access through a stable door.

Often it is left unfurnished long after lambing, until a sudden emergency galvanises us all into action; perhaps the arrival of visitors whom we don't know well enough to ask to eat in the kitchen. It has also served as a sitting-room for Hungarian refugees and it has countless times been used as a repository for surplus furniture, which I have acquired at sales.

This weakness of mine causes Johnny much despair, as we have no room for it, and the furniture will be stored in the back kitchen until I have disposed of some of my other junk. There it remains for weeks or even months until the necessity to reclaim the room for other uses forces poor Johnny to stagger to the barn with wardrobes and chests of drawers, to his own accompaniment of an unprintable running commentary.

Once, while it was a dining-room, it became an impromptu stable for Sunshine, Johnny's mare, who wandered in through the open door one hot summer's day to escape the flies and discovered with relish my lovely fuchsias and geraniums in pots on the windowsill.

CHAPTER 5

Mrs Stevens

We settled in at Nethercote Cottage for our first winter while the builders were busy at West Nethercote. The boys came home from school for the holidays and the girls joined us from Cornwall with Minouche, a French girl who was looking after them. We were somewhat cramped, since the cottage had only a double bedroom and two small singles, and a small kitchen and sitting-room. In addition to Arthur and Minouche we had Beatrice (known as B) with us. She was a friend who needed a change from working in London and had come to help Johnny with the farm work.

Eight of us slept at the cottage. It was just as well that our armchairs and sofa had been unable to get through the door, for our double bed got no further than the sitting-room. The four children were in the double room and Minouche and B had the two singles. Arthur slept in the empty, dust-clouded West Nethercote and joined us for meals.

The top of the oak refectory table, bought from the previous owners of the farm, rested under the window, balanced on two oil drums because its base was too wide for the doors. We all gathered round this makeshift arrangement for meals, some of us sitting on a long bench and others on the double bed.

There was a cooking stove run on boiler nuts called a

'Cook and Heat', which I called my 'Kick and Hate' because I couldn't cope with it at all at first, having been used to an electric cooker in Surrey. It was quite a job cooking for nine in the little kitchen and my activities were further dislocated by the fact that I had continually to go backwards and forwards between the cottage and West Nethercote, where our farming activities were based.

We lost no time in buying a dozen young cockerels and fattening them for Christmas as presents for family and friends. Inevitably, the day came when we had to kill and dress them. I had never plucked or drawn a fowl, so Arthur volunteered. He wrung their necks while I kept well out of the way and he did most of the plucking, inadequately assisted by me. I was very slow. Arthur was quite quick, though he could hardly be described as fairy-fingered, and I suppose we both grew more slapdash as hour succeeded hour. The result was that patches of the birds' skin came away with the feathers and they presented a mottled appearance, as if they had survived several rounds in the cock pit before succumbing.

We dressed them after a fashion (our own fashion) and placed them on a slate slab in the dairy at West Nethercote. Later that day I happened to go over to see Mrs Stevens and behold, there were her fowls ready to send away. I gazed at them, goggle-eyed. Their smooth unblemished breasts lay gleaming at me in rows; their wings were folded neatly under them with their legs trussed up, the stumps of their necks hidden in a fold of skin and the small slit through which she had extricated their innards was neatly concealed. Each work of art, decorated with a sprig of parsley, was enclosed in a cellophane wrapper.

'Have you finished your poultry?' she asked me.

'Yes,' I muttered, praying she wouldn't ask to see it.

29

She didn't. She fixed a time with me for her to come and show me how to salt a pig. She had had one of her pigs killed and sold us half of it. It was cut up into various anatomical sections, some suitable for hanging up in the corners of the fireplace to be smoked for bacon or ham, the rest to be salted and kept in our huge wooden pig salter in the dairy until required.

Of course I hadn't bought nearly enough salt, so Mrs Stevens brought her own.

As my lesson was to take place in the dairy, where the salter was kept, I cunningly covered my poultry with sheets of newspaper. I trembled during the whole of my period of instruction lest she should ask what was underneath. To my relief she didn't and finally I got her safely out of the room and on her way home. I escorted her as far as the front door and was making my speech of thanks when she suddenly remembered her salt, left in the dairy. I volunteered at once to fetch it, but Mrs Stevens is very sprightly and she beat me to it.

The salt was on the windowsill, so she had to pass right by my guilty secret. As she did so, she whisked off one of the sheets of newspaper asking 'What have you got under here?'

My shame was spread out before her eagle eyes. She was speechless at first and so was I, of course.

She groped for something to say and in the end she managed to get out, 'Ah, I see you've done your poultry.'

I was a coward and blamed it all on poor Arthur.

Mrs Stevens is also the Queen of the country wines and we have often savoured the delicious varieties she conjures forth like elixir. She saved me once from losing face. When our friends Dot and Reggie arrived on a visit to our Exmoor fastness, the first thing I did when they walked in was offer them a drink. We happened to be rather well supplied and I reeled off the choice at their command; just the usual things, sherry, gin, whisky, etc. Before I was half-way through, Reggie cut me short, and to be awkward, announced, 'I'll have some parsnip wine, thank you.'

He thought he had me stumped, but I agreed at once, without batting an eyelid. I nipped over to East Nethercote as fast as my legs would carry me and, sure enough, Mrs Stevens came to the rescue. I was soon back with a bottle and it is one of the rare occasions on which I have got the better of Reggie.

There were many village functions organised for charity, or for raising funds for a new village hall, and soon after we arrived Mrs Stevens asked me to contribute something towards the refreshments for one of these events. I hadn't yet sorted out my jumble of kitchen utensils, some of which had been left in the garage by the removal men while others were over at West Nethercote, so I had my recipe book, but not my scales.

Nonetheless I decided to make some iced buns in the 'Kick and Hate', because they were what I had christened 'the recipe that never fails'. No matter what I did to them, or omitted to do, they were always delicious. Having no scales, I guessed my quantities and placed the mixture in trays in the oven. When I thought they should be done I opened the door to look at them.

This moment of my discomfiture coincided with the arrival of Bill Saunders. He was then the postman at Winsford, father of eight children and evidently used to lending a hand in the house. He brought our mail every morning from the village. He also took away any letters for posting, since our nearest letter box was at Larcombe Foot, at the end of the lane, almost two miles away. He cycled or walked many miles daily to outlying farms, some of which were inaccessible except on foot or horseback.

Mr Saunders waltzed into the kitchen, to see me standing in dismay before the mess in the oven. The mixture had overflowed madly out of each little round mould and was spread in a sticky mass all over the trays.

'What has happened?' I gasped.

'What has happened,' he answered calmly, 'is that you put too much sugar in your mixture. The same thing happens with my cakes if I overdo the sugar.'

I was filled with respect and admiration for this masculine prodigy, who went on to inform me that making the week's cakes for the family was his regular Sunday enjoyment. He gave me a few useful tips before he went on his way.

The next time Mrs Stevens approached me about refreshments for the Saturday night dance she asked me if I would give a trifle. This was more ambitious and I pored over Mrs Beeton, anxious not to fail. I was appalled by her list of ingredients; the dozens of eggs, blanched almonds, sponge cake, sherry etc. I slaved for hours with the limited material at my disposal and produced at long last a quite creditable trifle, which she greeted with amazement since she had meant a small sum of money, probably thinking this offering would be preferable to my culinary failures.

In due course we bought a house cow and Johnny taught me to make clotted cream. Every morning, in the empty back kitchen at West Nethercote, I scalded the milk on two guttering and smelly little oil stoves left behind by the outgoing owners.

He also taught me how to make butter from the cream, stirring it round and round by hand, clockwise, in a big round wooden vat. Butter can't be made in a warm kitchen and it is no good trying to make it on a hot summer's day, even in the cool dairy. The best time to make it is in the early morning. If the outside temperature is too warm you can go on turning and turning the cream until your arm and wrist ache and your back is breaking and nothing happens. The butter won't 'make' as they say, or, if it makes, it is so soft that you can't shape it.

I was caught several times that way to start with. The first occasion was when my father and my sister Niki came to stay on their first visit from Cornwall and I decided to show them how the miracle was achieved. I had had no trouble before, so I was unprepared for disappointment; but this time I went on revolving my right hand round and round, and then my left, until half an hour had gone by and I was red in the face. I kept assuring them that any second now they would witness the most wonderful sleight of hand by means of which the cream would suddenly separate into two components, butter and buttermilk, but in the end I had to give up.

There is nothing like farm butter, but it soon goes, for we all spread it so thickly on our bread or toast. It takes me about three-quarters of an hour on average to make three or four pounds, from the time I start until I am ready to scrub the empty vat and utensils in boiling water. I haven't the slightest doubt that more practised farmers' wives can do it in half the time. Mrs Stevens is such an expert that she can judge half a pound to a fraction of an ounce and her finished pats all weigh exactly the same. This is important if you are selling it, but we don't, and my slabs of butter are all shapes and sizes.

CHAPTER 6

The Master Mechanic

When we bought the farm our land consisted of 250 acres, some 50 of which provided rough grazing. This was a steep hillside covered with gorse and bracken, known as the Brakes, much of which was too steep to be ploughed and seeded with grass, though Johnny has since reclaimed part of it. The rest was divided into fields of roughly six to ten acres and was entirely pasture land. With the exception of the meadows by the river, most of it was rather thin pasture.

Nearly all the fields needed to be ploughed up, treated with fertiliser and re-seeded. The farm was overgrown with weeds, which gradually had to be eradicated; the hedges had been neglected and there were so many gaps in them it was impossible to keep our sheep in any one field – they had the run of the farm. Most of the gates were broken down and it was a struggle to open and close them; many weren't gates at all, merely hurdles which had been placed across a gap and tied with binder-twine.

On the whole the farm buildings were good, apart from the pigsties. We took over the farm implements at valuation. Some were good, but most of them were rather antiquated and we had to make do with them until, gradually, we could afford to replace them with more modern ones. Our Fordson tractor cost us £80 and did yeoman service for many years.

This was the tractor which, one Sunday morning, Johnny drove down one of our steep fields called Brimmy Cleave. It ran away and he jumped off just as it turned the first of several somersaults before landing the right way up. Whereupon he drove it home, undamaged except for a bent exhaust pipe. A neighbour, who happened to witness the scene from the far side of the valley, walked over that afternoon and told Johnny his mother would have said that was what came from driving your tractor on a Sunday.

We had an old-fashioned grass cutter, on which I spent many happy hours when we cut the meadows for hay. It required two people to manipulate it; one to drive the tractor, while the other sat on a precarious perch on the mower behind and yanked a lever which raised the blade to avoid molehills and large stones, and when it was necessary to turn to start cutting a fresh swathe. You had to judge to a nicety the moment to drop the blade again at the beginning of the new row and I really enjoyed this, in spite of the occasional husbandly reaction when I mistimed it.

I loved working outside with Johnny. It took me away from my household chores and made me feel I was being a proper helpmeet to him, though looking back on it I suspect he found me more of a hindrance than an asset. Nowadays we have a modern cutter which one person can manage and my services are no longer required.

In the same way, in the early days, I would drive the open Jeep round a bumpy field while Johnny sat perched on the back of it, sowing grass seed with a fiddle. Now that we are more highly mechanised I am no longer required for this job either and I miss the fun. And not only the fun, but a certain bond that our close co-operation created between us. We were both in it together, we were sharing in the work and it made me happy and proud. Now we each have our own work, his outside, mine mostly indoors, and it isn't the same thing. Only during lambing time do I come into my own and I wouldn't miss a lambing for anything in the world.

A fiddle is called a fiddle because it looks like one. It consists of a small canvas bag into which the seed is poured and to which is attached a stick like a violin bow. The sower walks along the furrows plying this bow to and fro, to and fro, like a fiddler, always at the same pace so that the seed is sprayed out evenly. Before the fiddle was invented the sowers used to walk along the rows broadcasting the seed by hand and some old farmers still do it; that is how Johnny learnt to sow as a boy. Now the fiddle itself has been superseded by an attachment to the tractor, so he only uses it in fields where it is impossible to use a tractor.

Johnny found walking up and down a field all day sowing very tiring on account of his bad leg (a legacy from his wartime crash), which is why he decided to do it from the back of the Jeep. Our first experiment with me as driver didn't go entirely to plan.

He gave me a pep talk before we set off and impressed on me that I must concentrate on driving at a steady pace, gently, in bottom gear, to allow him to distribute the seed evenly. He then disposed himself with his back to me, so that even if the noise of the engine hadn't drowned his words I still couldn't have heard what he said.

I was feeling nervous because my driving efforts usually failed to reach his standards, added to which the field was crossed at intervals by shallow trenches, making driving smoothly difficult. Timorously I crept forward like a tortoise. Almost at once I heard a yell, so I trod hard on the brake and did an emergency stop, stalling the engine.

'What the hell do you think you're doing?' greeted me in the sudden silence as Johnny picked himself up from the floor of the Jeep.

It turned out he had shouted at me to go a bit faster. With grim determination I set off again and soon came across one of the ditches. I drove the front wheels into it at my slow even pace and realised with trepidation that I should have to accelerate to get up the other side. Down went my foot on the accelerator and out we shot, with the fiddle flying through the air, having been jerked from Johnny's grip.

The explosion behind me was terrible and reduced me to a jelly, although I couldn't hear what he said, mercifully. Sweating with apprehension, I resumed the even tenor of my progress until we came to the next ditch.

I crawled down into it too slowly, with Johnny yelling, 'Go on! Go on!' because he was fiddling away and all the seed was falling in one place.

I was afraid to accelerate too much after my last experience, so I released the clutch with my left foot and pressed so feebly on the accelerator with my right foot that, just as a roar of 'What the hell are you waiting for?' reached my ears, we stalled once more.

Fortunately I improved with practice and ended by enjoying it.

On another occasion when Johnny was sowing a field with grass seed I was allowed to chain harrow the part of the field which he had already sown, while he went on fiddling the unseeded part. This meant I had to drive the tractor up and down, towing the chain-harrows behind it. We set off after breakfast up the steep track leading to the top of the farm, known as Great Leys lane. Johnny went first on the tractor and I followed in the Jeep, the back loaded with large sacks of grass seed, with Arthur perched on top of them and the fiddle on the floor.

There was a gate at the bottom, and after I had passed through it I had to stop for Arthur to jump off and close it. The handbrake didn't work, so when he had climbed on board again I released the footbrake slowly and accelerated like mad to stop us running backwards. We started off with a colossal leap, which precipitated Arthur and the sacks into a heap on the floor.

When we reached our destination, I set off on the tractor while Johnny unloaded the Jeep and made his fiddling preparations. I had to harrow the middle of the field and I got on like a house on fire, with none of the usual horrors which beset my efforts. I was full of the joys of spring as I saw Johnny walking towards me across the ploughed field. He shouted something at me but my hearing, now very poor, was already troublesome then and the tractor was deafening.

I managed to make out, 'Go on with the middle.' So I nodded, grinned at him cheerfully, and drove on, unaware that his actual words had been, 'You've broken my fiddle.'

Next time I passed him he was still standing there for some strange reason, inspecting his fiddle, and he called out, 'You've ruined the end of it,' which I interpreted as, 'You're doing splendidly.'

So I waved at him happily with the world at my feet and was about to sail past him, holding my head a little higher, when to my amazement he shook his fist at me. I pulled up and the truth came to light; it was my flying start in the Jeep which had done it. When he subsided I bowed my diminished head and continued on my way, a somewhat chastened helpmeet.

I suppose it is hardly surprising that Johnny prefers me to peel potatoes. In any case he believes that no woman can be trusted with any mechanical device, that if a key won't turn she will force it until it bends and that if she can't unscrew something she will hit it with a hammer. He keeps his tools hidden away, but this doesn't prevent him from accusing the whole family of having mislaid them when he can't find them.

'Where's my grip wrench?' (as if I knew what it looked like). 'I definitely left it in the tractor box. You must have used it and left it lying about. How can I ever get any work done on this farm when all my tools are borrowed and then lost?'

So I drop everything and hunt around until I find something on his workbench which looks as if it might be able to grip if not to wrench, and take it to him hopefully. It turns out to be pliers or an adjustable spanner and I hear a few home truths about my intelligence quota as compared with that of a normal child of three. I have time to notice, before slinking back to the kitchen, that he is using a peculiar instrument which I subsequently discover to be the missing grip wrench, which had been in the tractor box all the time, hiding under a lot of other tools.

Still, there are compensations. There is absolutely no need for even the slightest bit of nagging when something goes wrong with the electric blanket or the bedside lamp or the alarm clock. All I need to do is to walk unconcernedly into the presence of the Omniscient One carrying a screwdriver, some flex and some insulating tape, plus the deficient object and, once seated, casually apply the screwdriver to the affected part. In less time than it takes to say 'IQ' it will have been snatched away and the Master Mechanic will be at work, no matter what 'vital jobs' he had in mind.

CHAPTER 7

Leader and Minky and Alby Ridd

We have had many wonderful dogs. The best of them all were Leader and Minky, who came with us from Surrey. We have sheepdogs now, and terriers, and we love them too, but no dog can ever take the place of those two Labradors. Leader was yellow and Minky black. Both were gentle and neither of them had an ounce of vice although, as happens even in the best families, each disgraced us from time to time.

Minky couldn't resist the temptation to chase people on bicycles and bark at them until they lost their nerve, wobbled and fell off; then she retired satisfied. Leader left Romeo in the shade and would make his way to the village, where he would sit all night outside someone's house waiting for the appearance of his Juliet. If his patient vigil went unrewarded he didn't depart empty-jawed but removed a love token from the unconquered citadel in the form of any shoe or boot which he found in the porch or by the back door.

Thus a missing wellington would be discovered on a neighbouring farmer's dung heap and its brother in the girls' cloakroom of the village school, and he concealed PC Short's boots so successfully neither of them was ever found. This was an expensive amusement for us and one which didn't exactly endear him to the people of Winsford, until they came to recognise his noble nature and forgave him his little eccentricities.

Leader left other dogs alone, provided they understood from the outset that he was the master and they his underlings, entitled only to second pick and expected to surrender to him at once anything which he fancied, even if it was a newly caught rabbit. Usually he succeeded in imparting this on sight to other dogs, by telepathy, and they accepted it without challenge. Occasionally he encountered one who was unimpressed and had to be shown. He would then advance upon the other fellow and in a flash, and with a neat flick, turn him over on his back and bite one of his legs. As a rule he never had to repeat the lesson.

With the farm we inherited three sheepdogs and sixteen cats. Leader and Minky made instant inroads into the feline population, giving up in despair after they had disposed of five and still more kept on popping up under woodpiles and in mangers. One of the dogs, Shep, had owned the place for several years before we arrived and naturally he regarded Leader as an interloper. He welcomed Minky with alacrity. This didn't suit Leader at all, for although he had a roving eye Minky was his mate and he would have died in her defence. As a rule he was charm personified with humans, but I have seen him hurl himself with teeth bared at a man who threatened her with a pitchfork.

A few warning growls and stiff-legged advances having failed to dampen Shep's enthusiasm, Leader gave him the leg-bite treatment. Unfortunately the leg became septic and Shep had to spend three weeks at the vet's. When he came home there was never any more trouble between him and Leader, but I regret to say they ganged up on Toby, Victor Stevens' dog.

Toby, while of a nervous disposition, was gentle and affectionate and anything but aggressive. His nervousness made him growl at Leader, who decided to subdue him. So he turned him onto his back. When I arrived hotfoot in East Nethercote yard in response to Toby's frantic squeals I saw that Leader, instead of gripping his victim by a leg as usual, had him by the throat and was shaking him. I waded in and struggled to prise open his powerful jaws.

Mrs Stevens and Victor were away from home, but another Exmoor farmer happened to be in their yard. He continued to stand there, watching the Punch and Judy show, until I succeeded in parting the dogs. Then he unconcernedly walked away. By that time Toby, terrified and defending himself with his fangs for all he was worth, had given me 14 bites on my right hand and wrist. Within a couple of days my arm was like a balloon and my temperature 104. I ended up spending nine days in bed with blood poisoning.

Toby was none the worse for his ordeal because, as it turned out, Leader had only had him by the loose skin of his throat and had barely punctured it. But at the time I thought he might kill him and it never for an instant occurred to me I had any choice but to try to save him.

Yet when I later discussed the drama with Mrs Stevens, she declared, 'You were mad to intervene – you should have left them to get on with it.'

'I thought Leader might kill your dog!'

'So what?' she remarked laconically, 'You wouldn't have been bitten, nor got blood poisoning as a result, and there would have been one dead dog, that's all.'

Leader and Minky were our beloved companions for many years. Leader would welcome the members of his family by taking their wrists between his teeth and pulling them gently along. Minky took between her teeth not people's wrists but their hens or goslings and brought them to us as presents, depositing them at our feet unhurt and without a ruffled feather.

Leader was still playful and full of vitality when, at the age of 12, he died of phosphorous poisoning, contracted heaven knows how. Minky, his devoted comrade for so long, kept vigil by his body in the garden while Johnny dug his grave in the Splat, the meadow below the house. When he came back to fetch Leader he found his body half covered with loose soil from the flower bed. She had tried to bury him.

Minky died at 13 and is buried in the Splat beside Leader. Their paw marks were imprinted side by side in 1952 in the wet concrete of our doorstep.

The farm was overrun with rabbits and watching them play was a joy to me. They were no joy to Johnny, who viewed them with a farmer's concern.

Arthur also loved seeing them, for a different reason. His expression was almost beatific the first time he saw our fields and spotted dozens of rabbits scuttling for cover wherever he looked. In Surrey, he used to go rabbiting with a friend and there would be great rejoicing when they bagged one after several hours' hard work with dogs and nets; if they ever caught two it was a major triumph.

Nethercote was Arthur's idea of paradise. He spent every spare moment stalking rabbits with Shep and his gun and I forget how many he claimed to have killed with a single shot. It was certainly an all-time record. He was a good shot and never failed to replenish my larder during the first year or two. Later, when the rabbits were less plentiful, he occasionally had the mortification of returning empty handed after we had clearly heard a couple of shots. Poor Shep, whom he used for retrieving, invariably got the blame. 'The obstinate old bastard,' (I am forced to misquote him) would keep on getting in the way just as he was about to fire.

Apart from shooting them, Arthur also set wire snares for them or bolted them with ferrets. He had brought his ferrets with him and life at Nethercote was wonderful for them too. His pals came down from Surrey on holiday and the fun was fast and furious. I had no problems about dog food and we ourselves had rabbit for lunch two or three times a week.

This was all very well, except that preparing them took some time. Of course it never entered my head to paunch them myself; I expected the men to do that before they dumped them outside the kitchen door. But I did learn to skin them. Once shown, it was simple. It's just like peeling off a glove by turning it inside out.

Soon there came the day when half a dozen bunnies were deposited at my door unpaunched. I left them there all day, hopefully, and we had a makeshift meal. In the evening Johnny paunched them, but told me to watch because it was quite easy and the men hadn't time to waste on jobs which were my province. This 'province' of mine has so increased its limits in the past ten years that if it were territorial I should by now figure among the landed gentry.

Johnny was alarmed by the great number of rabbits on Nethercote and realised what a tremendous amount of grass they were consuming, which could otherwise be feeding sheep. He reduced their number by every means in his power, short of gin traps which we abominated. We looked on them as barbaric instruments of torture and we never altered our opinion of them, although in the end we were forced to use them. At first we hoped to control the rabbits with snares and ferrets, but these methods were mere drops in the ocean and they went on multiplying.

We were visited, that first winter, by a couple of professional rabbit trappers, who asked for our custom and assured us that we would never be able to farm on Exmoor without trapping. We were adamant and refused their services.

The wide strips of bare earth along the hedges and on the banks, where the rabbits had eaten all the grass, went on spreading, and since they are no respecters of boundaries the creatures invaded our neighbours' land. They all trapped of course, using gin traps, which was the accepted method and the only effective one, but the more they caught the more new ones arrived from Nethercote. We realised, sadly, that we should have to fall into line.

The gin trap is cruel because it doesn't always kill a rabbit outright, by closing its steel jaws on its head. Usually it snaps shut on the poor creature's leg and it struggles desperately to free itself, thus enormously increasing its suffering. In most cases the leg is broken and the rabbit suffers for hours before the trapper arrives to put it out of its torment. Trappers are supposed to go round their traps at regular intervals every few hours and many of them did, but some left them alone from early morning until dusk – and even a few hours is a terribly long time for an animal to be in pain. I would never go far from the house when the trapper was with us. The sight of the poor things still alive in the traps would have sickened me. I knew I would have to knock them on the head and I couldn't face having to do it.

Although I kept away it was impossible to pretend it wasn't happening. In the stillness of the evening we could hear the rabbits screaming as they were caught. When they were brought home for the table I had to skin them with mangled legs and bleeding heads. I had to steel myself to do it, not because they looked so messy, for I'm not afraid of blood, but because of the inescapable realisation of what they had endured.

When myxomatosis, horrible as it was to behold, finally exterminated the rabbit population altogether in our part of the world I was infinitely thankful. At last we would no longer have to endure the gin traps. Much as I had once loved watching the rabbits at play I never wanted to see another. For several years we were completely free of them. They have started to come back, but they are few in number. Long may it remain so.

The year after we moved to West Nethercote, 1952, a trapper called Alby Ridd caught over 3000 rabbits in six weeks.

Alby took up his quarters at the farm, sleeping in the hayloft and having his meals with us. He had been trapping ever since he was a boy and there was nothing he didn't know about the ways of rabbits and the best places to set his traps. He would set them in the evening and go round at first light the following day, collecting the rabbits and resetting the gins. He inspected them again during the day and once more at dusk. He had plenty of work on account of their numbers.

Alby was a young Hercules, terrifically powerful, and would tramp down the hill to breakfast in the morning with his night's catch draped in pairs over his head and shoulders and hanging from his arms. He had the candid mind of a child and was very proud of his great strength. I think his biggest catch in a single night was 163 and I took a photo of him standing in our yard carrying this huge load and looking like a fur covered Eskimo. They must have weighed well over two hundredweight. He was delighted with the photo and carried it about in his breast pocket like a talisman.

He had no 'book learning' and writing was a laborious effort, but he had a splendid head for figures and his memory was fantastic. We paid him so much per rabbit and he could tell Johnny faultlessly how much he was owed, not only for one day's work but for weeks back, without ever jotting down a figure. He would know exactly how many rabbits he had trapped on any given day in the last three weeks.

Alby was a great character and very popular with the whole community. It was a shattering blow to us all when he was killed on his motorcycle early one Christmas morning, when he ran into an Exmoor pony on a moorland road.

He played the accordion and the mouth organ and was always delighted to give us a tune. He never left the table after lunch without obliging. He would hold his mouth organ in both hands, with one hand held upright against his cheek and the fingers pointing straight up to the ceiling and his eyes would dart right and left over his fingertips as he played, glancing at his audience.

With his childlike candour he loved appreciation and would always wait anxiously at the end of a meal for us to ask him to play. Occasionally, to tease him, we said nothing.

He would wait eagerly for a while and then his hand would go to his pocket as he asked, 'Would you like a little tune?'

He had a considerable repertoire and many is the time

when a certain tune has reminded me of him – particularly one of his favourites called 'Mocking Bird Hill'.

Sometimes he would dance for us, wild flings and Russian-type dances which enchanted the children and their friends from Surrey who were staying with us; or he would run across the yard to show us how fast he could run. When Johnny took him up the farm on the Fordson there were many gates to open and he would leap off the moving tractor and race ahead uphill at breakneck speed to open the gate before the tractor reached it.

He enjoyed life tremendously. He loved bright clothes and when he dressed to go out of an evening after his day's work he would appear in the kitchen for our appraisal in a vivid canary shirt, a flaming red tie with a girl's picture on it, his hair liberally sprayed with 'California Poppy', and his inevitable bottle-green beret. This he always wore. Our daughter Hilary made him a splendid pompom for it out of multi-coloured wool and he was thrilled. When he lost the pompom out trapping he asked her to make another and she did.

He often had time to spare during the day, between his trapping rounds, and would beg to be allowed to do the washing up. He said it was his favourite work, apart from rabbiting, and he really did seem to enjoy it. I needed no persuasion. Another job he vastly enjoyed was cleaning the silver and copper. We have many copper dishes and vases and ashtrays, which I brought home from Cairo; these take hours to polish and kept him busy to his heart's content. There were also my mother's enormous copper saucepans and frying pans from her French home and the kitchen table would be piled up, as the hours went by, with glittering utensils gleaming in the lamplight.

I wasn't allowed to remove them as they were polished; the whole grand collection remained there in full view for everybody to admire. They had to wait for Johnny to come in from work and I couldn't lay the table for high tea until he had suitably expressed his wonder and astonishment.

Alby's eyes would glow with pleasurable anticipation and he would repeat from time to time, 'Mr Johnson *will* be surprised!'

CHAPTER 8

First Lambing

We put the rams in with the ewes in October, soon after we arrived at Nethercote. The gestation period is five months, so by mid-March we were getting our first lambs.

We made the final move from Nethercote Cottage to West Nethercote at the end of March, in such a snowstorm that our furniture, on an open trailer, became coated with snow on its short journey. That night conditions worsened and Johnny went out with Shep and a storm lantern and gathered all the ewes with young lambs, and those ewes who were likely to lamb in the night, and brought them indoors. None of our outbuildings were available as we had horses in the stables and at that time our barn wasn't considered safe for sheep; in previous years several had died of an infection called blackleg after being shorn in there and we had been warned not to use it again until it had been thoroughly disinfected.

We couldn't use the back kitchen as an emergency shelter as it was cluttered with the furniture which had been brought over from the cottage that very day, so Johnny drove the sheep in through our new kitchen and into the room next to it, which had formerly been the parlour and is now his office. We were kept awake for the rest of the night by the choral symphony from the ground floor. The room wasn't yet furnished, but since then I have sometimes had to roll back the carpet in a hurry when the back kitchen has been full of ewes and lambs and Johnny had a particularly tricky obstetrical job to perform.

Our first lambing was a terrible ordeal.

With the farm, we had bought a flock of Exmoor Horn breeding ewes. There were 90 ewes and two rams, an Exmoor Horn and a Dorset Down. One of the former owners picked out for us those ewes which he considered suitable to be put to the Exmoor Horn ram, turning the remainder into another enclosure. We assumed this meant all those in the second enclosure could be served by the Dorset Down. In fact a number of them were young two tooth ewes which he had kept back because they were the Horn ram's daughters, to avoid in-breeding, not because they were suitable for the Dorset Down ram.

It was our first encounter with the Exmoor Horn breed and we didn't know, either, that they can have trouble lambing, particularly two-tooth ewes, which haven't lambed before. Dorset Down rams have a large head, and to make matters worse the winter of 1951/52 was mild, with plenty of keep, so the ewes carried big lambs.

A lamb which is coming the right way should arrive head first, with its head resting on its two front legs. The first thing you should see is two small black hooves with the nose resting between the forelegs. Then the ewe gives another heave or two and out pops her offspring. With young ewes carrying big lambs with large heads it was a different matter. In many cases their pelvises were too small and the lamb remained jammed in the uterus. Or, if it got down into the passage, the latter was too narrow to accommodate both head and forelegs together.

The result was that a head only would emerge, with the legs left behind, and at least one of them would have to be found and gradually inched out before the lamb could be born. With a big old ewe, who has been stretched by many lambings, it may be possible to deliver a 'head only' presentation without getting hold of the legs; it is hopeless with a young two-tooth. The legs get firmly wedged and you would injure her very seriously if you attempted to pull the lamb out by the head.

Alternatively, the legs would appear without the head which, having no room, would be bent backwards from the neck and securely jammed. Johnny would be obliged to insert his hand to try to sort out the tangle, while I held her still. His hand is large and the narrow passage, blocked by the lamb's body, made it almost impossible for him to get it in, let alone perform any manipulation. The ewe would cry out with pain every time he tried, and yet he had to try for she could never lamb without help.

Sometimes he would ask me to have a go with my smaller hand, but I felt helpless because I had no idea what to expect to find. I could only just insert it, and once it was inside I had no room to move it. I would feel lumps and bumps and slithery flesh, which I would describe to Johnny as best I could and he would tell me what to feel for.

Once I had to grope for a lamb's leg which was bent back at the elbow, hook my forefinger into the crook of the elbow and pull slowly and gently in an attempt to straighten it out. At last I succeeded, but there was a sickening snap as the leg came forward. I had broken it at the knee. Johnny splinted it and the lamb survived, but the poor mother died. Perhaps she had been lacerated internally by the sharp little hoof as it sprang forward, or perhaps she had just been badly bruised by our efforts to help her and had contracted blackleg.

Lambing crises such as these are enough to put off any aspiring sheep farmer for ever more. Of course they aren't always happening. That first lambing was an awful experience for us and one for which we were totally unprepared. Since then, although there are always a few bad cases every year, things have gone smoothly on the whole and we really look forward to lambing time.

Johnny wasn't at first as expert as he is now, for it was years since he had worked on a sheep farm. Nowadays he easily copes with some of the difficult cases which defeated him at the beginning. Many of those cases he knew to be beyond his skill from the outset and he would load the ewe into the Lancia and take her into Dulverton to the vet, or the latter would come out to us as soon as he could reach us on his busy round, for there are calls on him round the clock during lambing time and I have known him arrive at Nethercote at 1.00am, white-faced and exhausted from his long day's work.

The first Caesarean operation I saw performed on a ewe was done on our kitchen table. The ewe lay on her back with her hind legs lashed to the bar fixed to the front of the Rayburn and her forelegs held by Hilary. It is a fascinating operation to watch and wonderful to see the lamb, or lambs, emerge alive and kicking. Later I was to watch the same vet perform a Caesarean section on one of Mrs Stevens' ewes and produce, like a conjuror, a strong, healthy set of triplets.

It can be that it is too late by the time you realise the ewe is in trouble. If, for instance, the lamb's body is already in the mother's passage and the head has emerged into the light of day, a Caesarean is useless. If all attempts to get the lamb away by hand fail, there is nothing for it but to knock it on the head, take a sharp knife and cut its head off. Then you can reach in and ease out the rest of the body. Johnny has been obliged to do this distressing job at times. Sometimes we are relieved to find a second lamb, tucked in behind the first one, which is born without trouble and greeted joyously by the ewe.

If a ewe gives birth to a dead lamb it is particularly important to see that she licks it and gets to know its smell; for almost certainly you have a lamb which you are rearing on the bottle – we call them tamies – which needs a mother. To persuade a ewe with a dead lamb to adopt a stranger, you do your best to deceive her. You take her dead lamb away out of sight and skin it. You then have a little jacket with which you cover the other lamb to fool her into thinking it is hers, pushing its legs into the empty sleeves.

Some ewes, particularly those who never heard their own lamb bleat, can be completely deceived by the jacket stratagem, especially if you first rub the lamb's head with it so that it smells familiar. They welcome the impostor with delighted crooning and nuzzling. As soon as they hear it bleat they bleat happily in response – a paean of praise and thankfulness. Their lamb, which they thought was dead, is alive after all. The adoption is instantaneous and it isn't long before you can remove the jacket.

Other mothers aren't really taken in by the small Jacobs which we try to pass off as Esaus. They know the lamb which has just been brought in to them isn't really theirs.

The ewe thinks, 'This can't be my lamb for mine is dead; yet it smells like my lamb … oh, if only it could be my lamb how wonderful it would be. But I know it is dead, I stood guard over its dead body for hours. This one can't be mine … but it smells the same. I do so want it to be mine … well, I think it must be,' and she begins to lick the familiar coat and make small sounds of greeting.

She isn't really deceived. Her intelligence tells her the truth, though the similarity in scent defeats her powers of reasoning, but her maternal instinct is stronger than her knowledge. She so badly wants a lamb she deceives herself.

It isn't always that simple. We once had to persuade a mother who had just had a stillborn lamb to accept a rather active substitute, already several days old. We tied its left foreleg and hind leg together and put it on the ground next to her, where its ineffectual struggles to get up made it look more like a newborn lamb. As soon as the ewe had licked it we removed the string.

CHAPTER 9

Lost Lambs and Staddy

Ewes and lambs can pick each other out by their voices among hundreds of others. Often the whole flock has to be gathered together, either to be moved from one pasture to a fresh one, or when we are tailing the lambs or castrating the ram lambs, or shearing. At such times the lambs become separated from their mothers and they have to find each other. It is one of the most satisfying experiences I know to stand on a slight rise, in a big meadow, and watch this procedure.

Perhaps the ewes have been waiting in the meadow, calling for hours, while the lambs have been penned up in the barn or in the outdoor run. Then they are released and turned out to join their mothers. A perfect pandemonium of bleating is let loose, deep notes replying to falsetto ones. There may be 300 ewes and 400 lambs in the meadow – though as a rule we try to deal with them in smaller batches.

Each ewe and each lamb unerringly knows the bleat of its own, and although they can't see one another in all that mix-up, and several acres often divide them, you can pick them out from your eminence and watch them gradually drawing closer until, suddenly, the lamb is able to recognise its mother by sight. Up until then it has been advancing rather hesitatingly in the right direction, with its ears cocked. Now it sees her and puts on a burst of speed, its little legs pounding the turf like a racehorse. It reaches her and dives under without stopping, butting her udder as it sucks until she is almost lifted from the ground.

We have learnt, particularly Johnny, to recognise most of our ewes and the lambs which belong to them, so that it is easy to reunite them if they have wandered too far apart. Johnny, like every shepherd who knows his flock, can single out a favourite ewe; Beauty for instance, or Penny or Welsh Mountain or Fluffy. He can pick out from the flock not only this year's lamb, but last year's and that of the year before last, if we have kept them for breeding purposes.

Johnny always does a round when the sheep have settled down for the night, to be sure there is no lost lamb or anxious mother bleating. Even so, it is impossible to prevent accidents. A mislaid lamb may have curled up for the night against another ewe, who will not object to its company but won't allow it to suck; then she may set off to graze, followed by her own lamb, leaving the other behind. Johnny will have heard no bleats of distress on his evening round, but he will find a dead lamb on his early morning one. No longer curled up as if asleep, it will be lying stretched on its side with its head thrown back, an unconscious gesture when they are nearly dying.

Sometimes a lamb will be lying like that, stiff to the touch and apparently lifeless. Any inexperienced person would swear it was dead. But there is still a faint heartbeat and it is possible to revive it. Its immediate need is warmth. You give it a quick massage on the spot, pop it inside your coat against your warm body and hurry with it to the house.

I have put a dying lamb (and make no mistake, it really is dying, you snatch it back from death) into the bottom oven of the Rayburn, leaving the door half open for air. More often I place it in a box with a wrapped hot water bottle beneath it and another bottle behind its back, and tuck a light woollen covering over the top of it.

Soon you notice a faint stirring as its heart begins to beat more strongly and find, on feeling the lamb, that the stiffness is disappearing. You turn away to get on with an urgent job, and all of a sudden there comes the sound of a small bleat. The little corpse has raised its head. This moment is one of my greatest rewards.

Having revived and fed the lamb, the next job is to find its mother. This can be a wearisome process and take up valuable time, during which other things may be going wrong. Johnny ought to be on his rounds, on the look out for lambing cases which may require urgent attention, and yet the mother must be found. Occasionally all his efforts have been fruitless and the lamb joins the tamies in the back kitchen, if there are any; if it is on its own we have it with us in the kitchen so it won't be lonely. As a rule it isn't long before we get it adopted.

If we have more than one lamb in the pool and we need one for a ewe, we make a point of giving her a ram lamb. This is because we don't want to be left with a ram lamb on our hands as we already have our quota of rams for our flock. If we don't keep him, he has to be castrated and sold, as a wether lamb, for slaughter. Whereas if we are left with a tame ewe lamb it can join the flock of breeding ewes.

It does happen, though not often, that we are landed with a ram lamb tamie. Staddy was such a one.

Since it was out of the question to sell him to the butcher, we decided to keep him as a ram and use him with the ewes when he was old enough to join the other rams. He was a very devoted little fellow. Johnny and I had had so much to do with him when he was young he always looked on us as his father and mother. He would come running up whenever he spotted one of us in the distance and follow us all over the farm. When I had time I took the dogs for walks and it was quite a circus for we were joined by Staddy and by Titbits, a foal of Hilary's.

Staddy came to associate the Jeep with Johnny and would tear after it. As he grew older he developed into a fine young ram and could gallop like a racehorse. One day Johnny drove the Jeep up over the farm and out onto the road to Exford. When he stopped to open the gate leading to the road, several fields away from where he had last seen Staddy, there he was, right behind him. He shut the gate in his face and proceeded along the road, but when he looked round he was still behind, going like a stag. Johnny was obliged to stop and take him aboard and they marched together into the bar of the White Horse.

As he matured, Staddy grew more and more aggressive. He wasn't afraid of people and afforded them scant respect, with the exception of Johnny and me, whom he never molested and always treated with affection. No-one else was immune from his attacks. B, our land girl, had left by then and been succeeded by Tommie, an SRN who had come to us for a change from nursing. He would chase her across the yard and into the kitchen; panting, she would slam the door in his face as he crashed his horns into it.

The children would sometimes organise a game of cricket

at the bottom of the Splat, but from the moment Staddy arrived on the scene they had to pack up. If Johnny or I were at the wicket he would watch our faultless drives with the admiration they deserved, but if any of the other unfortunates were batting he would run at the wicket, head down like a bull, and the bat never connected with the ball because its wielder had to use it in self-defence. Johnny and I thought this was very funny although nobody else did, understandably, since he could really hurt.

Eventually we decided the time had come to take him up over and leave him with the other rams, without much hope really for we were sure he would be down again before we were. We thought if he was taken up in the evening he might settle down for the night. Tommie was detailed for the job and showed a remarkable lack of enthusiasm. But she didn't have to drive him up. She ran uphill ahead of him and he charged from behind, driving her to ever greater bursts of speed to escape his horns.

The next morning Johnny found him dead, with his neck broken. The other rams were very peaceable and always got on well together and we could only conclude that Staddy had attacked them, and, being still young, was no match for them.

CHAPTER 10

Sheep are just like humans

For our first few lambing seasons we used to let the ewes graze in the fields up over during the day. Johnny went on periodical tours of inspection and every evening he would bring down into an enclosure near the house those ewes who were expected to lamb shortly, driving up again the following morning those who hadn't lambed. In the night he would get up for another tour of his lambing pen.

We discovered after a year or two that the ewes seemed to do better if we left them to lamb in their natural habitat in the fields at the top of the farm. They would then settle down comfortably in some favourite corner, tucked in under a hedge, and lamb happily with no trouble. Some ewes lamb in the same place every year. We do occasionally lose a lamb, which might have been saved if the mother had been near the house and had been seen in the night, but for every lamb we lose we reckon we gain on balance.

Johnny has become almost psychic in knowing when a ewe is likely to have trouble. He will tell me he thinks one or other of them is going to lamb in the night and that he doesn't like the look of her. He will then bring her down so that he can keep an eye on her. His instinct is almost always right.

The crows are one of our chief scourges. Their methods are bloody. If a ewe has a lamb which doesn't get up at once she may leave it lying unprotected while she moves away a little to have a second one; the crows, which are always hanging around on the watch, then peck out its eyes, as they will those of a grown sheep which is too sick to move, or a sheep which has got on its back and can't turn over again.

When Johnny is driving or riding up to the top of the farm at lambing time and he sees a flock of crows rise up from a certain spot at his approach he quickens his pace, for he knows what to expect. By the time he reaches the stricken lamb it is usually too late, they have done their foul work, and if it isn't already dead he has to kill it. Scores of times he and Arthur have stalked the vile birds, with their guns at the ready, but they seem to have a sixth sense and keep out of sight.

The alternative is to poison them, which is a terrible risk to take when you have dogs about. Even if you place a poisoned egg well out of their reach, or tie some poisoned meat to the branches of a tree, the chances are the crows will drop a piece as they fly off and a dog will pick it up.

A neighbour came to us one evening and told us that the crows had killed yet another of his lambs and he had decided to leave the dead lamb out as bait for them, with a dose of strychnine in its guts. He said the lamb would be right at the top of his farm, more than a mile from our house, but we must keep our dogs in that night and not release them until he had removed the bait in the early morning and given us the all clear signal.

The next morning, early, no signal had come. Johnny needed Lassie, our sheepdog bitch, to walk round his lambing ewes with him in case there was one which required catching, when he might need her help. Since she is absolutely obedient, and he wasn't going to let her out of his sight for an instant, he decided to take her with him. He was walking out with her into the yard when he was distracted by strange sounds coming from a pig ark a few yards away, where a sow had farrowed unexpectedly, and went across to make sure she was all right. This only took a few seconds, but in those few seconds Lassie had gone.

He whistled, but there was no sign of her. So he jumped into the Jeep and drove all out towards the field where he knew the poisoned lamb to be. Snow was thick on the ground and there came a point where it was quicker to get out and leap a hedge than to drive round. As he cleared the hedge he caught sight of her in the distance, busily devouring the lamb.

He yelled 'Lassie!', not in anger but in fear, but she took it as a reproach and ran off, her tail between her legs.

Meanwhile I was in the kitchen, getting breakfast. Lassie arrived home and I wondered why Johnny wasn't with her. Then she settled under the table and I thought no more of it.

Suddenly Johnny came panting in and gasped, 'Is Lassie here?' He had tracked her through the snow. When I nodded he cried, 'Quick, some mustard and water!'

We poured this down her throat and phoned the vet while we waited for her to be sick, in an agony of hope and despair. He said the only thing we could do was to make her vomit and that he would come at once, but that strychnine acted quickly and if she was going to die she would be gone before he could reach us.

She wasn't sick, so we pushed lumps of washing soda

64

down her throat, followed by more mustard and water. At last, after what seemed an eternity, she brought everything up. Never have I been so thankful to see my kitchen floor in such a mess.

Soon afterwards the vet arrived and told us that almost certainly some of the poison would still be in her system and that strychnine causes convulsions which are a terrible strain on the heart, and on the whole nervous system of the victim. In his opinion she would weather them better if she was unconscious when they came and he therefore proposed to give her an injection which would put her right under for several hours. This he did and we laid her on a sofa.

She had several attacks of convulsions, dreadful to watch, one of which threw her onto the floor. But she was right out and knew nothing. When she came round they had passed and she was dazed but otherwise normal.

We were extremely lucky not to lose her. We heard of a gamekeeper who took his dog with him one day on a round of his pheasant hatcheries. The dog picked up a bone with some meat on it. His master wouldn't allow him to eat it while they were on their rounds, so he carried it in his mouth. As soon as they reached home, his master gave him a pat and said, 'Good dog. Now you can eat it.'

Within a few minutes, the dog was dead. The vet happened to be on the spot but there was nothing he could do. The meat had been poisoned.

When people say sheep all behave alike they make a big mistake. They have their own individualities, just like humans. We used to have a beautiful Exmoor Horn, called Cleo because she had two lovely curling horns which reminded us of Cleopatra's headdress. You couldn't mistake her, she was a queen among sheep. Every year she had a splendid pair of twins, so fat they could hardly waddle, she did them so well.

It wasn't only her rich milk that was responsible. The very first year she lambed, she discovered the feast to be garnered from the vegetable garden. No matter what we did she would find a way in with her twins, which she reared on spring greens, young lettuce and the tender shoots of green peas and broad beans. Year after year she repeated this cunning move with her new twins and Arthur, who looked after the garden, hated the sight of her. Johnny and I commiserated loudly, but secretly we felt rather proud to have such a clever old Cleo. Then one day Tommie found her dead up over. Her genius for clearing any obstacle in her path had killed her. She had forced her way through an impassable hedge and must have bruised herself, for she died of blackleg.

Fly-by-Night was another hedge hopper, whom no fence could hold. We would see her in the evening in one field, at the extreme western end of the farm, and by the next morning she would be as far east as she could get. She flitted at night across our farm, and across East Nethercote as well, flying hedges like a witch on a broomstick. We never knew how she did it for we never saw her. During the day she would graze quietly, like a proper stay-at-home.

Betty was even worse than Cleo. She would leap straight into the air and land on top of a 5ft high wall, without touching it anywhere on the way up. Even as a tame lamb it had been impossible to keep her out of the garden; she used to clear the wall, followed by all her friends, and gobble up the grape hyacinths and wallflowers and polyanthus. After devouring the flower borders she would lead her gang into the kitchen garden, where they dealt with the emergent seedlings.

She spent the summer up over with the other sheep and we were lulled into a false sense of security. For hardly had autumn merged into winter when she appeared in the yard, ears pricked, eyes expectant, nostrils twitching.

What did Johnny do? Ignore her? Drive her off and shut a gate behind her? No, he was delighted to see her and rushed up the steps into the barn calling her urgently, grabbing a handful of sheep nuts to tempt her with. This performance was repeated daily and Betty soon learnt to jump over the stable door into the barn and help herself to pellets, nuts, cow cake, hen corn, crushed oats etc, turning the bags inside out, while Johnny kept on telling us how clever she was. She lambed in the garden and produced a ram lamb who levitated vertically just as easily as she did.

In the winter, when there isn't much grass, and in the spring when the ewes are in lamb or feeding young lambs, Johnny supplements their diet with Ewbol, special sheep pellets which they simply love. As soon as they see him arrive with the bag they all tumble over one another to reach him. If they are out of sight he has only to whistle and they come running. I have often seen him drive round the farm in the Jeep, followed by a mass of sheep and with others rushing up from the more distant fields to join the throng.

This performance on the part of our sheep once paid dividends. Our Bank Manager, approached for an increase of our overdraft, elected to inspect the farm to satisfy himself about our methods. Johnny took him up over in the Jeep and when they reached the top he whistled and the sheep came running like the rats of Hamlyn. The Manager was terrifically impressed. He told me later over coffee that it was the first time he had met a farmer whose sheep were so well-trained he didn't need to use a dog and merely had to whistle.

He was delighted to raise our overdraft ceiling. But Johnny felt, rather guiltily, that he had pulled a fast one on his sheep by deliberately leaving the bag of delectable pellets behind.

CHAPTER 11

Visitors

Creatures have been born all over the house; lambs in the back kitchen and the office, kittens in the kitchen, puppies in our bedroom – and mice everywhere. I wage a perpetual losing battle against mice, for as soon as I get rid of one lot, another arrives. They are field mice and nest in the walls, burrowing in from outside and invading the house. We simply have to accept them as part of the farm and make the best of it. But they took some explaining to my German cousins, who came over from Bavaria to stay with us filled with Teutonic notions of cleanliness and hygiene.

The poor girls had some dreadful shocks in store. One of them once glimpsed a cow's hair floating on the milk in the milking pail and drank her tea with lemon from then on. She always removed her shoes before entering her bedroom, never sat on her bed and hung her sheets out of the window to air every single day. As soon as she realised that our bread, far from being delivered to the back door wrapped in cellophane, was left by the baker in our box at Larcombe Foot and brought up bouncing around in the back of the Jeep, she singed every loaf on the calor gas cooker.

Her sister, although equally fastidious on arrival, adapted herself more readily to farm life and grew to love it. We enjoyed having her and she spent eight months with us, learning English and helping me with my various chores. She was unused to dogs in the house and told us that in Germany they were usually kept outside, but she cheerfully mopped up the little pools and packets with which the lambs and puppies decorated the kitchen floor.

Our sheepdog, Lassie, had her first litter on our pink taffeta eiderdown. It has never been the same since. The first puppy arrived on the bedroom floor during the night. Johnny thought Lassie was uncomfortable down there and needed warmth and reassurance, so he carefully lifted her onto our bed. When she had finished, and was contentedly licking the row of little brown sausages which were sucking lustily, we settled her back on the floor on a rug.

I found it would cost at least £10 to have the eiderdown recovered and my budget couldn't rise to such an extravagance. So I scrubbed it as best I could and put it away in the zinc-lined blanket chest. But it has to be disinterred and pressed into service when there are visitors and we are short of bedclothes. On such occasions I give our guests our least shabby eiderdown and a member of the family is treated to the one on which Lassie whelped.

We often use Gillian's room for our visitors, since it is convenient for the bathroom. Two little accidents happened to it early on. Although Johnny intended to do something about them, somehow the months went by and turned into years and he was always too busy. So our visitors get used to the room's peculiarities.

There was (and still is) a panel kicked out of the bottom of the door, leaving a space just wide enough for Gillian's terrier Crumpy to pop her head through and inspect the inmates. I do try to jam the broken panel back into position, but Crumpy or the draught are apt to precipitate it into the room with a clatter in the early hours. The other oddity was a gaping hole in the ceiling, where our son Peter once fell through from the loft.

When my cousins Jane and Francis came to stay with us they had Gillian's room. This was their first visit and it must have been quite an experience for them, though they have since become acclimatised. At midnight, as they were undressing for bed, I suddenly remembered the delicious concoction they were supposed to have enjoyed for high tea – a lemon whip which was still reposing in the larder. This was a special delicacy in their honour as we never have a sweet when *en famille*, and I had completely forgotten it.

I bore it up to the bedroom in triumph, with spoons for its consumption, but forgot the plates. So we all sat on the threadbare red carpet in dressing-gowns and dipped into the bowl, while above us, through the ceiling, peeped the corner of an old mattress and half a cardboard box with Christmas decorations trailing over the edge.

Down through the years drift echoes of Miss Faithful's voice. She was headmistress during some of my time at Cheltenham and used to give the senior girls what she called her 'Saturday talks'. One of these was on the subject of hospitality. She told us what a guest should expect to find in a well-appointed guest room; flowers, of course, and a good selection of lavender scented towels, a gleaming set of brushes and combs and a hand mirror, soap, talcum powder, toilet water (cosmetics weren't mentioned, they could be of no interest to schoolgirls of the 1920s), a spare razor and toothbrush, writing materials and clean blotting paper, and a list of the times of church services.

How sadly she has been let down by one of her old girls.

But I always remember the flowers. My sisters and I never fail to put a vase of them, however small and inadequate, in our visitors' bedrooms. We call them our little fiddledeedees – and they *are* very fiddly at the last moment, when you are in a flat spin and can hear the car approaching.

There are other irregularities at West Nethercote, to which the visitor has to adapt. The bathroom floor has sunk, for instance. The bolt on the door no longer meets the groove into which it should slide. It is no good moving the bolt since the floor keeps on sinking and it would need constant readjustment. Unless something is done, one day the bath will descend into the kitchen below. Some of our guests are quite alarmed and, I believe, hang on to the towel rail with one hand while they scrub with the other, and the rot has spread so that even one or two faint-hearted members of my own family are affected.

In order to secure the bathroom door against intruders it is necessary to open the top part of the airing cupboard and jam it against the door. But sometimes the airing cupboard opens on its own because the latch is faulty. Then, if someone doesn't know the tricks of the trade, they try the door and can't get in, so wait patiently for the non-existent occupant to emerge.

When my Scottish friend Nora came to stay with us we had the following conversation.

'I'm afraid I couldn't make the plug in the lavatory work.'

'Oh Nora, I'm so sorry, I forgot to tell you. The handle doesn't function. There is a piece of wire sticking out of the cistern and you give a yank on that and it flushes. Really the simplest thing would be for you to use the one in the bathroom and then you'll have no trouble.'

'Well, I thought of that but I can't get in. There seems to be a wee door inside, which is pressing against the bathroom door.'

'… Ah, I must explain. You have to take a knife and slide the blade along the top of the outer door until it comes in contact with the edge of the inner door and then you push and the inner door will close and release the outer one. A comb or a knitting needle will do just as well as a knife.'

Poor Nora nobly refrained from comment but I noticed that she refused coffee and drank no second cup of tea.

The bathroom has become a haven to most of the family, particularly Johnny. It is the only place where we have time to read and, indeed, where we can do so undisturbed. There is always a pile of literature on the floor, to the amusement of our guests.

There is reading matter for every taste and it is possible for a caller to guess who is at home by inspecting the assortment. There will be copies of the Farmer and Stockbreeder or the Farmer's Weekly, usually outdated, plus the Sunday paper; then there is probably a half-finished crossword puzzle and a copy or two of Woman's Own. In the school holidays there is sure to be a Georgette Heyer or some soul-searing romance, while during university vacations there may be anything from a treatise on missionary work in the Philippines or a book on chess tactics, to a volume of Greek tragedy or the voyages of Marco Polo.

From time to time I have a wholesale clearance and scoop them all up from the floorboards, but they soon accumulate again.

Over the years we have had people sleeping in odd corners all over the house; on the landing behind a screen, in rows in the back kitchen, on cushions on someone else's bedroom floor and, one summer, our four children slept in the straw in the open Dutch barn. For months afterwards Johnny and Arthur forked up odd gym shoes and magazines and torches with the litter for the bullocks.

Once during the summer holidays we were 14 for a week and 17 one night for bed and breakfast. The house was filled with young voices and laughter, for our cheerful guests were friends of Stanley's from the boys and girls schools at Sherborne. They slept on mattresses and camp beds and old iron bedsteads hauled down from the loft. They snatched their food in the kitchen in relays and all lent a hand with the work, washing up, gathering vegetables and fruit, peeling potatoes, stringing beans and so on. I was able to sit back and relax.

They even built a bridge for us across the river out of old doors nailed to tree trunks. We held a solemn opening ceremony and I christened it the *Pons Asinorum*; but when Johnny came to inspect it he failed to display the appreciation expected of a good host and gazed at it in that silence more eloquent than words. Despite his reservations it withstood several gales and spates, though it has now been swept away and only a dangling door is left, hanging drunkenly from a tree stump.

We had enough menfolk that weekend for a cricket eleven which played the Exford village side. There were several new faces which the local inhabitants didn't know and one of them was heard to ask another where they had all come from.

'I believe they are the Johnsons' house party,' was the reply.

I laughed when I heard this. What visions the words 'house party' conjure up.

CHAPTER 12

More Visitors

I'm afraid our poor visitors have often been treated in the most shocking fashion and it is a wonder they ever come again, but they have strong constitutions and seem to enjoy it.

Once, when Dot and Reggie were visiting Exmoor again and staying at the Crown at Exford, I invited them to dinner. By the time they arrived I thought I had asked them to drinks and we were in the middle of high tea in the kitchen, so I gave them drinks in the middle kitchen and asked them to excuse us while we finished our meal. Later we all went together to the Royal Oak at Withypool and they tactfully sneaked out of the bar one by one to have some food, while the others kept me engaged in talk so that I wouldn't notice one of them was missing. I didn't find out the truth until years later.

Another time I asked some friends to drinks at least a fortnight ahead and then forgot all about it. When they arrived Johnny was out and there was no fire in the middle kitchen, which was lit by a solitary, rather dim, oil lamp, the others requiring attention. It was twelfth night and the children and I were taking down the Christmas decorations. They walked into the gloomy cold room to find us standing on chairs, trails of bedraggled tinsel and paper garlands dangling mournfully from every beam, and the armchairs full of prickly holly and coloured balls from the tree.

I was completely thrown by their unexpected arrival and realised with dismay that we had used up our stock of drink over the Christmas festivities. Luckily I remembered a bottle of sherry and one of port, which had been sent up with the groceries. Quickly I fetched them from the larder and set out our dark green Cairo glasses. Apologising profusely for the lack of choice, I poured out the sherry, for which they had opted, and we raised our glasses to toast the new year – only to discover that the contents were meths, which the grocer had poured into an old sherry bottle.

Johnny walked in just as the port turned out to be meths as well, so we whisked them off to the pub and made amends as best we could. They were charming about it.

My *cri de coeur* on the occasion of the first visit of new neighbours, Mr and Mrs Webb, has become a standing joke between us. They had just bought Lyncombe, the farm two miles further up the valley.

Johnny informed me late one morning that Mr Webb was coming over in the afternoon to talk business and that he had asked him to bring his wife, 'So you'd better have something prepared for tea.'

It was one of the times when I had no domestic help at all. Nor had I any cakes or anything fit to offer and I am not one of those efficient females who can turn out piles of dainty sandwiches in a twinkling. I decided to make some oatmeal biscuits. As soon as we had finished lunch I prepared the mixture, leaving the washing-up and feeding the poultry. There were no flowers in the middle kitchen and I went into the garden in my working clothes and apron to pick some. As I was stooping over my task I heard the Webbs' car drive up. I was wearing odd shoes because one sandal strap had broken, my dress was grubby, my hair a mess.

It was impossible for me to get upstairs to repair the ravages without running into the visitors, whom Johnny was conducting into the middle kitchen. I ran back into the kitchen, doubled up so they wouldn't see me through the window, and flung my handful of flowers onto the table. Then, dragging off my apron, I made my entry, greeting our new acquaintances with as much poise as I could muster.

With the introductions over, Johnny and Mr Webb settled themselves in armchairs at one side of the room and Mrs Webb and I were left to entertain each other at the opposite side. We talked and talked and we went on talking; we exhausted every subject we could think of. Still the men sat there in earnest conversation. At one point I excused myself just long enough to pop the oatmeal mixture in the Rayburn. Then Mrs Webb and I grimly continued our probes into each other's families, travels, tastes and habits. At the back of my mind raced disturbing thoughts of hungry hens, the washing-up and the waterless flowers on the kitchen table.

Finally Johnny, as he and Mr Webb got up, interrupted our flagging efforts by announcing, 'Darling, I'm just going to show Mr Webb round the farm for an hour or so.'

Something snapped. Out came my memorable appeal in a thoughtless rush, 'Oh, *do* take Mrs Webb too!'

Luckily she burst out laughing. She stood not upon the order of her going. Liberated, I hurried to the kitchen, to find the fire almost out, the oven barely warm and the mixture unrisen. In the end I was obliged to cope with sandwiches after all, for it was 6.00pm before my biscuits turned the right shade of gold and by then they were like stones.

Most of the people who come to stay are friends who have come from afar and therefore expect to remain a few days. We treat them as members of the family, who are free to come and go as they please and whom we make no effort to entertain. The best are those who occupy themselves, exploring the countryside and leaving us to get on quietly with our jobs. We are glad to have them with us; they know that we will always push them in somewhere and that they are welcome whenever they care to turn up.

It does happen, however, that people sometimes propose visits at awkward times. We make it a rule never to have anyone during lambing, but there are other times when it seems churlish to put them off and yet Johnny may be particularly busy with shearing or haymaking, or I may be short of help and tired. When we have had a number of visitors in quick succession we both feel we would enjoy having the house to ourselves for a while.

Johnny says, 'Thank God! That's the last of the visitors and now perhaps I'll be able to get some work done. If you dare have any more this summer I'll divorce you! I might as well go off and get a job and you can turn Nethercote into a guest house.'

Then, within a few days or even a few hours, the phone will ring, or I will get a letter asking if so-and-so may come for a day or two on their way to Cornwall or home from Wales.

I simply cannot bring myself to say no, and having said, 'That will be lovely. We can't wait to see you,' I don't know how to break the news to Johnny.

For there is no avoiding the fact that a continual flow of guests interferes with the routine of the farm – quite apart from the effect on our rocky finances. We are expected to sit talking over the breakfast table; I feel I should make the effort to produce coffee after meals and I shelve urgent chores. The more sedentary among the visitors tend to buttonhole us with inquiries and endless stories; friends wander into the kitchen to chat and I can't think what I'm supposed to be doing, or they trail out into the yard and engage Johnny in conversation, just as he's trying to cope with some tricky mechanical adjustment to a piece of farm machinery. This is one of his worst bugbears, together with having small boys demanding rides on the tractor and asking endless questions.

Then, since the farm lands are very steep and it is a labour for people to climb up to the top on foot, Johnny feels he ought to take them in the Jeep. He enjoys showing them round when he can spare the time, but often he can't. However he is charm personified to our visitors and nobody would guess what a carry-on there is before they arrive and, sometimes, during their stay when he catches me on my own.

He will ask me repeatedly when they are leaving, pretending he doesn't know and saying, 'They're off tomorrow, aren't they?'

I answer, 'You know very well they're staying till Monday next.'

Whereupon he gives an exaggerated start of dismay and exclaims, 'WHAT? You don't mean to say you have invited them for a whole week!'

Or else he will heave long-drawn-out, heavy sighs as soon as they are out of earshot, or just murmur, 'How long?' to me in a dying voice as he passes me in the passage.

I try to keep out of his way because, somehow, he manages to make me feel that I am to blame for all his sufferings. They become *my* friends, instead of our joint ones, just as the children are mine alone when they don't meet with his approval.

'How do your guests expect to get to the station?' he will ask, or 'Will you see that your visitors don't leave the engine running all night?' (The generator which we now have continues to run if a light is left on, consuming precious diesel.)

To have to sit at home in the evening making small talk isn't Johnny's cup of tea – a pint from the barrel is more to his liking. His friends are usually more than willing to help him find one, but many of mine are not pub addicts and prefer an evening by the fire. He can't face more than one evening of this and yet he doesn't want to appear rude. So I have a quiet chuckle over the excuses he invents for going out at night. He has to get some special bolts from the blacksmith for the tractor; the next evening he has to take them back because they are the wrong sort; the following evening he has to take a pig to Withypool to sell, and the one after that he has to see George Burnell about docking the sheep and he can't get hold of him in the daytime.

During the Christmas holidays of 1955 we had a teenage party at Nethercote, which I planned before the children came home from school and about which I wrote to them as follows.

The Crown Hotel is doing all the food for us, which will save a dreadful flap all day on the 27th. As it is, we shall have our hands full clearing the furniture from the rooms, lighting huge fires, etc. Already Daddy has expressed the hope that I haven't arranged a lot of social activities next holidays which will involve him in driving backwards and forwards, fetching food and collecting children, and stop him getting any work done! I haven't dared to tell him what is fixed up so far. Of course he knows about our party, but he keeps on pretending he doesn't and every time I mention it, he nearly jumps out of his chair with feigned astonishment and shouts, 'WHAT?' or, 'We're not having a party here, are we?' and then adds, 'Well, I hope you don't expect me to collect the food from the Crown Hotel.' Of course he knows quite well that he *will* have to collect it.

Or he says, 'Well, I don't have to be there, do I? You can manage quite well without me.'

I tell him I shall need him for carrying logs and keeping the fires going, and filling the oil stoves and entertaining the parents. This last bit always makes him groan loudly!

While it is only too clear that some of our friends have suffered discomfort and even famine at our hands, others have given us quite a rough ride.

On one embarrassing occasion a friend from New Zealand arrived with his car plastered with notices 'BUY NEW ZEALAND LAMB', right into the stronghold of English lamb producers. He gave me a lift, with his car thus bedecked, to the meet of the staghounds at Exford, where I knew we should run into the entire farming community. I slumped low in my seat, but was recognised by two riders who asked me the reason for this shocking display. Unnerved, I resorted to subterfuge and enlisted the help of Gillian, who was with us. While our friend was busy taking photos of the meet she crept back unobserved to the parked car, removed the offending labels and hid them in the hedge. Thus was face saved, with friendship unimpaired.

Worse than this, however, was when John and Dawn, friends from Surrey, wrote to ask if we would have their Labrador, Blimp, because John had been offered a job in Tanganyika and Blimp was too old for the African heat. Of course we agreed at once and they wrote back suggesting a date for a farewell visit to leave Blimp with us. They asked if they might bring with them their son James, aged two. The younger baby, fortunately, was to be looked after by Dawn's old nanny.

This was arranged, although Johnny looked forward with horror to making the young gentleman's acquaintance. They duly arrived with James, Blimp and a little bitch, unheralded, called Molly. But it turned out that John hadn't yet heard whether or not he had got the Tanganyika job, so they weren't going to leave Blimp with us as yet and had just come for a holiday.

James exceeded Johnny's worst fears. Poor Dawn had her hands full; two is a dreadful age for a small boy, since he is full of mischief but can't be reasoned with. John either slept all afternoon on the divan in Johnny's office or propped his feet on the desk and read a book; this was his holiday and James was Dawn's province. The little monster scattered soap powder about like snow, upset the ink and the paraffin stove, climbed on Leader's back, hit Lassie with one of the wooden batons on which I stand my milk strainer and finally fell out of the window.

It was funny to see Johnny smiling heroically at his parents and darting venomous glances at James when they looked the other way. John did bestir himself enough to take James into the Splat to stroke Staddy, but his idea of stroking was to bang him hard on the back; whereupon Staddy flicked his head round and butted him, sending him sailing through the air. John thought this a huge joke and roared with laughter, saying it would teach him a lesson.

We had made up beds for them in a room as far removed as possible from ours, but John refused to have James in their room because he would wake them up at an unearthly hour in the morning. So I put him in the next farthest room from Johnny, which was Hilary's. They had brought a cot, but informed me that he always climbed out of it and would probably pull down all Hilary's pictures and tear up her books. I suggested we put the deck tennis net over his cot to keep him in.

Dawn said this would be cruel, that he wouldn't be able to stand up in his cot and would scream and wake the whole house, and that she would feel awful if she was 'so unkind to the poor little chap.' I said she would feel much more awful if he broke and ruined all Hilary's precious things, and luckily John was on my side. So the deck tennis net was firmly tied into position by Johnny, who was determined to be sure the job was properly done. All was well. He didn't get out, he didn't scream, and we all slept peacefully.

Hardly had they settled in before the kitchen was littered with boats and woolly toys, the middle kitchen was strewn with bricks and the bathroom with face flannels, wet nappies and tiny shoes and socks. A trail of dogs followed Blimp and Molly all over the house, since 'my' guests never remembered to close the doors, and had high jinks in the bedrooms.

To Johnny's mutters of 'How long?' I had no answer, as they hadn't said. Eventually we discovered that they had arranged to collect their baby from the nanny in 11 days. Stunned, we hastily organised a visit to my sister Niki in Cornwall and regretfully announced our unavoidable departure, so they only stayed a week. John returned later to leave Blimp. But we all survived and have remained the best of friends.

Before they left, John and I had a most illuminating conversation.

He informed me he didn't want Dawn to become a hill farmer's wife and added in explanation, 'After all, I married her because she is attractive, and after five years on Exmoor she would look like an old frump.' (This shook me.)

He went on, 'Also, Dawn is quite witty and amusing now and after five years on a remote farm she would be hopelessly dull. I didn't marry her for that!'

'Well,' I said to myself, 'I know I'm no film star, but I didn't realise that I'm dull as well.' So I protested, 'I don't know, John. I think that if you have an amusing turn of mind you will always remain amusing, whatever your surroundings.'

'Oh, my dear old girl!' he hastened to say, 'Please don't take my remarks personally. After all, Dawn is young. One still expects her to be attractive. At your age, nobody could expect to find a ravishing beauty!'

Silence, I noted, regarding any pretensions I might ever have had to a small share of Dawn's wit.

CHAPTER 13

Tommie and Towing the Sunbeam

Tommie lingered on at Nethercote for three years before going back to nursing, too broken in spirit, I suppose, to summon the energy to leave. She must have found life with us more of a change than she had bargained for.

Her first drama occurred when she had hardly unpacked.

The men were shearing and we had some outside helpers on the job. Johnny had come over from the shearing shed and told me when to carry over tea, and had then set off to fetch down a fresh batch of sheep from the top of the farm. Tommie and her friend Betty (another SRN who spent a few weeks with us, but soon made her getaway) were catching the sheep for the shearers and sweeping away the locks, the odds and ends of soiled wool. Arthur was rolling up the fleeces and tying them.

As one of the ewes was being shorn she suddenly jerked her head and the shears slit open the side of her mouth and half her cheek. With blood streaming from the gash, the shearer let her loose among the other sheep, remarking without undue concern that he thought he had cut an artery and she would die.

Tommie came rushing over to the house and asked for Johnny. I told her he was up over and she shot away without telling me why he was wanted. Not yet knowing the farm, she had no idea that our land rose steeply to nearly 1300ft. She ran uphill like a hare for 20 minutes before she reached him, gasping for breath.

Meanwhile Arthur came to fetch me and I grabbed a needle, snipped some nylon gut from a trout reel and ran across to the shearing shed. There was blood everywhere, the other sheep were streaked with it. Betty helped me catch the ewe and I felt furious that it should be necessary for us to chase her; then she stitched her up expertly while I held her.

When Tommie returned with Johnny, still panting, it was to find everything under control and a cool reception awaiting her from me for having left me in the dark, since the ewe might have bled to death if Arthur hadn't fetched me. All Johnny had to do was to give her an anti-shock injection. She made an excellent recovery.

At least Tommie proved that day that she could run, and Johnny was unable to indulge in his usual ribaldry about the efforts to run of his female assistants. He compared Christa, a young Swiss friend, to a broken down carthorse, a three-legged tortoise and a donkey who has spent all summer plodding up and down the beach.

'RUN!' he will yell at them, 'Don't stand there gaping. Stop that sheep. Don't let it get away. Now it's got past you – what *do* you think you're doing? NO, it's no use chasing it, run *round* it. RUN!'

One day he asked Hilary and Tommie to fetch back two Kerry ewes which had got mixed up with Victor Stevens' sheep. It is a difficult job at the best of times to separate two sheep from a bunch of others, but Kerries come from the Welsh mountains and are very fleet of foot. The girls' activities were concentrated on a particularly steep piece of ground, up and down which they had to run in order to pick out the two Kerries from among the milling flock and head them away from the others. Finally they had to bring them down a steep stony lane between the two farms, called Fuzzball.

Johnny, when giving his instructions, always describes them as 'little jobs' which won't take very long. As a rule they turn out to be mammoth undertakings and the children and I have christened them 'Daddy's lesser jobs'. When the exhausted victim returns after a couple of hours, sometimes unsuccessful but invariably having strained every nerve and sinew, Johnny will announce that he could have done it himself in half the time.

On this particular occasion Hilary and Tommie managed at last to separate our two ewes from the rest and, staggering on their legs, drive them down the lane. As they reached the bottom of Fuzzball and were about to open the gate to let them through, one of the Kerries dodged past them and doubled back up the lane, jumping the hedge and rejoining Victor's sheep. While they were watching to see where she went, the other Kerry got away.

At that moment Johnny arrived to check up on their progress. He asked them what they imagined they were doing, flapping around in circles like a couple of useless old hens? Both girls sat down simultaneously on the bank and, simultaneously too, burst into tears. Then they saw each other weeping and started to laugh. Tommie later drew a cartoon of a farmer leaning idly over a gate, smoking his pipe, while two hens flapped about among some sheep, with feathers flying.

Tommie lent a sympathetic ear to many of my tales of woe

and I was able to laugh with her, later, over things which seemed anything but funny at the time. A dire misfortune becomes a joke when you have someone with whom to share it.

One January morning Johnny went off to Taunton market. I was in the middle kitchen later that afternoon when, through the window, I saw the most luxurious and enormous pale blue and black car drive into the yard and heard a hoot.

'Bother,' I thought, 'visitors.'

Tommie was in the kitchen, so I decided I would let her deal with them.

After a moment she came pattering along the passage and said, 'A car has drawn up in the yard and I thought I heard a hoot, but it's empty.'

We went out and there was the car, but not a sign of life. As we puzzled over this mystery a laughing figure emerged from behind the bulldozer. It was Johnny, who had been hiding there. He informed us he had bought the car, a colossal great Sunbeam with seats for six and a huge luggage compartment. He said he had had his eye on it for ages; they originally wanted £100 for it, but he had that day clinched the deal for £20.

I was enchanted. Here was a car roomy enough to take the whole family comfortably, with baggage to boot. I pictured us rolling across Europe on a lovely holiday. As things turned out, it did actually once convey all six of us to a point-to-point, chugging slowly and sedately uphill, rather short of breath. But it has been lying dismantled in the barn for the past three years, waiting for Johnny to find time to overhaul it.

A few days after its arrival it refused to start, although it had started perfectly in Taunton. Now the battery was flat and the generator wasn't charging. It needed to be towed by the tractor and, inevitably, Johnny had to stifle his misgivings and fall back on me for help, since Arthur didn't drive.

The Sunbeam was in the implement shed and the plan was that I should sit in it and steer while Johnny towed me out backwards into the yard with our Ferguson tractor (known as 'Fergy'). He would then be able to bring the tractor round to the front of the Sunbeam so that I (on the tractor) could tow him (in the Sunbeam) along the lane until such time as he managed to get her started.

I sat in the car and he showed me the brake and said she was in neutral and all I had to do was steer while he towed. I said a silent prayer and gripped the wheel staring fixedly ahead as Johnny, behind me, tied a short rope between us, mounted Fergy and started off. What he had omitted to point out was that the Sunbeam was jacked up on two big wooden ramps, which he normally uses for loading our bulldozer onto the low loader. These ramps sloped sharply downwards at the end. Therefore, no sooner did the vehicle start to move than its wheels ran onto the slope of the ramps and it shot back at a dizzy speed. Before I even realised what was happening the Sunbeam hit the tractor smartly in the rear.

'God Almighty, what ARE you doing?' Johnny roared at me.

Of course I wasn't aware that I had done anything, except sit there and do as I was told. He jumped off the tractor, fuming, glanced at the back of the car and came up to tell me that I had made a frightful mess of it (some paint was removed by the impact) and that he'd shown me where the brake was and why didn't I use it? Why did I think he had made a special point of showing me the brake?

Then he discovered I had run over the rope. He tugged at it, but couldn't release it and had to go off to fetch a knife to cut it. After that the rope was too short and he had to find another one. By then he wasn't exactly whistling merrily 'Oh, what a beautiful morning!' I was in a complete dither and dreading having to perform the next part of the manoeuvre. I had only driven the Fordson, our other tractor, and had never yet been called on to drive Fergy.

Johnny towed the Sunbeam as far as the top of a sharp slope down to the stream which runs between West and East Nethercote, over which we had built a low water crossing.

He then came striding back to me as I sat drooping in the driving seat and said, 'Jump out.'

I levered myself out, with doom in my heart.

He escorted me to the tractor and said, 'There's the brake, there's the clutch and here's the throttle. Now, all you have to do is to keep your foot on the brake, put the other foot on the clutch, put her in second and take care not to knock her out of gear with your skirt, take your foot off the brake, release the clutch slowly and away you go! Nothing to it. And when you want to stop, you put your foot on the brake first and then the other foot on the clutch, and you bend down and there's a little ratchet which you fix on the brake and you'll have to hold it there with your hand before you take your foot off, but I don't think you'll be able to reach it, and then you put her in neutral and take the other foot off the clutch and jump off. It's all perfectly simple. And those other two bars that you see in front of the clutch and brake are footrests. Got it?'

Needless to say I got nothing, except that the clutch was on the left and the brake on the right, which was strange to me, quite apart from the rest of the rigmarole, since the old Fordson had a brake and clutch in one. I put a brave face on it and in compliance with Johnny's command to 'jump on', I settled myself reluctantly into position for the take-off.

I placed my feet firmly on the clutch and brake, inspected the numbers indicating the gears, and listened to Johnny's final instructions about the various signals he was going to give with his arm and on the horn according to whether he wanted me to stop, go on, accelerate or slow down. Then he left me and moved back towards the Sunbeam.

As he stood for a moment inspecting the tow-rope before getting in I decided to put Fergy in gear, so that I would be quite ready to move when he signalled. My undoing was caused by the fact that whereas I imagined my feet to be reposing on clutch and brake, they were merely on the footrests. I shoved the gear lever into second, and as bad luck would have it, I got it in without using the clutch.

Instantly Fergy leapt forward in one wild kangaroo leap and went galloping downhill, heading for the stream, while I sat there, appalled, frantically pressing hard on what I thought was the brake to stop its mad career. Meanwhile I could hear Johnny roaring behind me like the bull of Basham. The Sunbeam had slewed round and was half-way down the steep bank on the right and nearly in the stream.

In the end I stopped the tractor, heaven knows how, and with my foot firmly on the brake I turned round, horrified, to see what was happening behind me. But I was still in gear. In order to twist in my seat I unthinkingly took my left foot off the clutch, secure in the knowledge that the other foot was on the brake, which would have been quite sufficient to hold the Fordson. While I was still facing backwards, the tractor gave another kangaroo leap and was off again like a thing possessed. This time, fortunately, the rope broke, so the Sunbeam wasn't hurled into the stream.

By then, my wits had quite deserted me. I grabbed the hand throttle with some wild idea of turning off the engine, but I pushed it the wrong way and we went charging on even more furiously, speeding up the hill beyond the stream in the direction of East Nethercote, with me frozen to the controls.

In the end I forced my paralysed mind to think and managed to stop. Then I had to face the onslaught from Johnny. I crawled down from the tractor, completely unnerved, and swore to myself that never again would I set foot on a vehicle which galloped off on its own like some sinister iron monster from Mars. I could take no more, and in the middle of Johnny's picturesque flow of words I stalked off into the kitchen with head held high and eyes smarting. I sent Tommie to take my place and she crept out like a whipped dog. She was soon back again for Johnny wouldn't allow her near the tractor.

So there was nothing for it but for me to have another go, since he couldn't possible extricate the Sunbeam on his own from the position in which I had landed it. Luckily for me, things went smoothly at last, and finally the Sunbeam's engine roared into action after some towing. I was able, with consummate skill and coolness, to turn the tractor at the bottom of the narrow lane and drive it home, with Johnny doing me the honour of riding on it while I drove. Connubial harmony was restored.

CHAPTER 14

Lynmouth Flood

Our first summer at West Nethercote, in 1952, was the summer of the Lynmouth flood disaster.

The rivers Lyn, Exe and Barle all rise some miles away on the heights of Exmoor, where the moorland forms a natural reservoir. The Exe comes down through the village of Exford, flows through the Nethercote valley and on to Winsford, before running south past Dulverton to reach the sea at Exmouth, on the South Devon coast.

It was the middle of a very wet August. There had been a torrential downpour and (as we heard later) an incredible volume of rain had fallen in a short time up on the moorland, sending the overflow tumbling down the three water courses until they were turned into rushing torrents, gathering momentum as they were joined by the surging water of other overloaded hill streams. The Exe and the Barle overflowed their banks and spread wide over the countryside, but the Lyn was contained between the walls of a steep gorge, so that a raging mountain of water hurled itself into Lynmouth, sweeping trees, cars and people out to sea and turning buildings into rubble.

Even the Exe, with more room to spread, became a roaring, seething wall of water, which came hurtling down from the moor. It swept away everything it encountered, bulldozing trees and flattening high earth banks topped by hedges, carrying away the tents of a scout camp, engulfing corn crops and village gardens and flooding houses in Exford and Winsford.

All was peaceful at home at 9.00pm on Friday 15 August, when Johnny set off in the van in which he had brought Bessie the pig and the poultry from Surrey. He was going down to Larcombe Foot to collect some sacks of cement which had been left there and pick up a plumber from Bampton, who was coming to us over the weekend to do some jobs in the house. He took Arthur with him to help load the cement; it was the last we saw of them for more than 12 hours.

I expected them back in half an hour. When they didn't turn up I didn't worry because I suspected they had gone on to Winsford for a 'quick one' in the pub, so I went to bed. It was quite dark by then and pouring with rain again, and I could hear the angry sound of the river coming up to me from the bottom of the Splat, as I imagined, for little did I dream what had happened in the short while since the van had departed. Time passed and I began to worry and went to the window to peer out, but could see nothing in the blackness.

The hours went by while I lay in bed, sleepless and straining my ears. All I could hear was the rain and the river. Then Tinker, the 17 year old sheepdog who had come to us with the farm, started to howl. It was the most mournful sound in that sinister night and it went on and on. He should have been sleeping in the back kitchen, with the stable door open so that he could go out, but the howls seemed to be coming from the direction of Arthur's room. Arthur's bedsitter was in a small building next to the farmhouse and had once been used as a laundry; we had replaced the copper boiler with a wood-burning stove. Builders were in the process of making a cesspit in its vicinity and the pit was dug, but not yet roofed over.

In the grey light of approaching dawn I made my way through the house, barefoot and in my nightdress. Tinker wasn't in the back kitchen. As I stood in the open doorway, looking at the curtain of rain, I realised the howls came from the cesspit. I ran through the downpour and gazed over the brink. Tinker was immersed in water, which filled the deep hole to within a few feet of the top. Only his muzzle was above the water.

I lay in the mud, inching forward over the edge until I could reach under the surface enough to get a grip on the thick ruff round his neck. It was a titanic struggle because the wet earth was slippery, so was Tinker, and he was heavy as well. I managed to heave him to safety and carry him to the shelter of the back kitchen. I fetched a towel and gave him a good rub down and he was none the worse for his ordeal.

By this time it was much lighter and, soaking as I was, I went to the gate into the Splat and looked over it towards the river.

There was no river to be seen, no bridge across the place where the river should have been, no lane leading to Larcombe Foot on the other side of the bridge. Just a vast ocean of turgid brown water, which had swallowed everything and was reaching two-thirds of the way up the meadow towards the house. The valley bottom, along which the lane ran, parallel to the river, was completely engulfed. We had some young calves in the Splat but they were safe, shivering on the higher ground nearer the house.

I ran upstairs and woke the children and we gazed, awestruck, at the amazing sight. We appeared to be totally cut off.

The animals had to be fed and there were no men to do it. The three oldest children were then 14, 13 and 12 – it was two days before Stanley's twelfth birthday; Gillian was seven. They were soon organised. Hilary had milked a neighbour's goat in Surrey, so she went off to do the milking. Peter and Stanley fed the pigs and hens while Gillian laid the breakfast table. Meanwhile I went across to East Nethercote to ask Mrs Stevens what she thought could have happened to Johnny, Arthur and the plumber.

But my guess was as good as hers. Her son Victor had been down to the water's edge to investigate. It was clear that the wooden railway sleepers of which the bridge consisted had been carried away.

The water had begun to subside and the twisted iron supports on which the sleepers had rested were breaking surface. We had no means of knowing whether the other bridge lower down, which spanned the Exe between the end of our lane and the main road, had also disappeared since the phone was out of order; we felt sure it must have.

The men finally turned up at 10.30am, having walked down from the top of the farm.

Johnny told us he had reached Larcombe Foot in the van without trouble. The river was running high, as it always does after heavy rain, but was well within its banks. They soon had the bags of cement loaded, collected the plumber and set off up the lane, homeward bound.

They hadn't gone far before, without warning, a wall of water, travelling down the valley like an immense tidal wave swallowing up river, river bank and road, came rushing towards them. Johnny shot the gears into reverse and fled backwards before it, but it was moving too fast and soon swirled around the van, swamping the wheels and lapping through the floorboards. All he could do was quickly back it up onto a piece of higher ground and hope it wouldn't be swept away.

They scrambled out and up the hillside, out of harm's way, and so back to the bridge at the end of the lane, which they had left only a few minutes earlier. But the great wall of water had already reached it and carried it away, like chaff on the wind.

Johnny remembered the calves in the Splat and was determined to try to reach them, although he feared our home bridge would have gone as well. Leaving Arthur and the plumber where they were, he made his way through the bracken of the steep hillside above the submerged lane until he reached a point opposite where the bridge should have been.

It was pitch dark by then and a turmoil of hissing water, tree trunks and debris was rushing past, well above the level of the bridge. Thinking it might still be there, under the flood, and that he might be able to wade across it to reach his calves, he stepped down into the lane, bracing himself against the tremendous force of the current, and edged carefully forward in the blackness until he reckoned he was on the brink of the bridge. Then he took another step and his foot went down into nothingness. Quickly he snatched it back and retreated.

Going up onto higher ground again, he went on beyond the bridge until he stood opposite the Splat, but could see nothing. He thought of giving one of his piercing whistles to let me know he was there, then decided against it since I wouldn't hear it against the roar of the water but the dogs, Leader and Minky, probably would and might attempt to swim across to him. So he retraced his steps to the place where he had left the van.

It was still there, with Arthur and the plumber inside. The water was eddying round their legs but had risen no higher. He crawled in, dripping wet, and thus they passed the rest of the night, with the van buffeted and lurching under the impact of huge branches, long sheets of galvanised iron and countless other large objects which were swept past.

As soon as the water had gone down sufficiently to expose the iron girders which had supported the bridge by the road they crawled over them on all fours. Then they went along the road in the direction of Exford, until they reached the highest part of our farm and could walk down over the fields to a welcome breakfast.

Later that day we walked along the high water mark left by the receding river and gathered some of the flotsam which had come down from Exford. We found a whole sheaf of bills and accounts from the office of an Exford firm, and subsequently returned them, but the blacksmith lost all his accounts and had no idea how many horses he had shod or what bolts and bearings and ploughshares and other farm requirements he had fashioned at his forge. We all had to rack our brains to remember the occasions on which we had required his services.

The saddler had his entire stock of harness and leather goods carried away and we found some of it on our banks. We also picked up garden tools, a wellington boot and a jar full of nutmegs.

Everybody had some fantastic tale to tell. The blacksmith's father at Exford, who was crippled with arthritis and slept downstairs in the sitting room, was alone, lying in bed. Luckily he was on a rubber mattress, for we were told that when the rescuers reached his home he was floating 18 inches from the ceiling and hanging on to a gas bracket. We also heard that a trout was found swimming around in someone's kitchen sink the next morning. There was certainly one splashing about in the middle of a pool on the Exford-Winsford road.

In Winsford, the ground floors of all the houses near the river were flooded and General Savery's chicken coops were swept away, with the birds inside. At the vicarage, parish records dating back centuries were under water, as were the vicar's books. It was a tremendous task to dry them out.

At Withypool, where the Barle burst its banks, people had to be rescued from their bedroom windows. We heard that one elderly lady was brought down by ladder wearing her Sunday clothes and her best hat – no doubt the simplest way of saving them from the ever-rising water.

For three or four days Nethercote was virtually cut off from the outside world. Victor Stevens and Johnny went over the hills by tractor until they came down into Winsford without having to cross the Exe. There they began to retrieve the missing sleepers from our two bridges, making their way gradually up river and easing them out from among the debris. Fortunately they were able to collect enough of them to repair the lower bridge near the road. They had to tackle that one first in order to be able to cross it with supplies for repairing the one near the house.

Our friends Dot and Reggie and their three children were staying with Mrs Stevens at East Nethercote and were isolated with the rest of us. It was a terrific adventure for them. The children were soon performing the most perilous acrobatics on the remaining bits of bridge and it was the making of their holiday.

CHAPTER 15

Pigs

After the disastrous night of the floods, which were particularly tragic for Lynmouth but which also seriously affected those living on the banks of the Exe and the Barle, a warning system was set up so that outlying farms near the river wouldn't be caught unawares. It wasn't long before it was put into action along the Exe.

One night after heavy rain the river began to rise alarmingly. A messenger from Exford ran a mile in the dark to warn the tenant at Lyncombe, the farm subsequently bought by Mr and Mrs Webb, which is up the valley from ours. The young farmer there knew we had pigs bedded down in pig arks in a meadow at the river's edge and ran the two miles on to us with a hurricane lamp to tell us. We were awakened by his shouts under our window.

Johnny hurried to the meadow with visions of drowned corpses, but although the arks were flooded, the pigs had had the sense to get out and make for higher ground. All were safe.

We haven't kept pigs at Nethercote for some years now, but in those early days we went in for them in a fairly big way, for us. The government was telling British farmers to keep more pigs, in order to produce more home-grown bacon and cut down on our imports. Accordingly we did so, in common with many other optimists. We were advised to market our baconers when they would fetch the best price, that is when they weighed between seven score and nine score pounds. After nine score they become too fat for bacon and the price goes down as the weight increases.

But what happened was that little or no provision had been made for an increase in the intake at the bacon factories. They were unable to cope with the glut of baconers. So we took our pigs to market, week after week, and had to bring them home again because there was a bottleneck at the factories and consequently no demand for them. The delay meant their weight soon passed the nine score maximum and their value decreased, while we continued to bear the cost of food stuffs and labour. Meanwhile the country was still importing Danish bacon.

The farmers lost heart, and no wonder. Most of those for whom, like ourselves, pigs were just a sideline decided to lose no time in getting out. The result was that the bottom fell clean out of the market. There were no buyers, only people wanting to sell. Weaners (piglets just weaned) which were worth £6 apiece were fetching £3, if you were lucky enough to find a buyer. Like many others, we cut our losses and sold out.

Since then, the market has improved, but we decided it was wiser for us to concentrate on our main products, sheep and beef, instead of distributing our activities over too wide a field. Pig-keeping requires a considerable amount of time and labour and we had none to spare.

The only pig we kept was our faithful Bessie, the sow who had lifted Johnny out of his seat on the journey from Surrey, and who had mothered innumerable large litters of fine sturdy piglets. In the end we were compelled to part with her, for she had grown old and heavy and become too clumsy to avoid treading or lying on the little ones. We couldn't afford the labour entailed in removing her litters at birth and bringing them to her to suckle while we stood guard. Nor would we have been able, in any case, to have hardened our hearts enough to have kept her apart from her babies. So reluctantly, and with great sadness, we sold her at Taunton Market with her latest litter and let her new owner cope with the problem of safeguarding her progeny.

Of all the pigs with whom I have become acquainted there was only one I couldn't take to, and that was Phoebe. We inherited her with the farm and she was not *sympathique,* as the French say. Phoebe had a mean look in her eye and was cussed and bad tempered. The usual Johnson approach, which seemed to charm our other animals into wholehearted co-operation, had no effect on her, probably because we hadn't handled her when she was young. One day she really made me hate her.

She was penned up in an enclosure near the yard, but had broken loose, unbeknown to me. In one of the stables there was a ewe who had lost her lamb, with a young lamb I had been trying to make her adopt. Unfortunately I had no jacket because one of the dogs had carried it off just after the dead lamb had been skinned and we never found it. The ewe had made up her mind not to accept the stranger and she and I had been having a battle of wills for several days.

At first I had had to keep her tied up because she was so hostile. Then I was able to release her without fear that she would injure the lamb, but I still had to hold her every time the lamb needed a suck. That morning, just as I had almost given up hope, she had allowed the lamb to suck unaided for the first time.

I was walking away, glowing with pleasure because it had all been worthwhile, when Phoebe suddenly burst into the yard and made a beeline for the stables. I called Arthur and we both ran back. We were too late to head her off and she hurled herself against the door of the loose-box, breaking through it as we panted up. She charged in, a few yards ahead of us, rushed at the lamb like the ravening beast she was, and tore it limb from limb under our eyes. I never would have believed it if I hadn't seen it happen.

After that, we packed Phoebe smartly off to market, with no regrets.

When talking about the 'whole-hearted co-operation' of our animals I feel that memory may have lent enchantment to the truth, for several other hectic incidents come back to mind in connection with the pigs we kept at Nethercote.

At one time we had no boar of our own and used to take our sows to one at Porlock, some 12 miles away. One day Johnny loaded two young sows into a trailer, battening them in with a roofing of wire netting secured by a tarpaulin. Then he and I set off, towing the trailer with the Jeep. We were bowling along, half-way to Porlock, when I glanced back and saw a pig's hind-quarters staring me in the face. The rest of her body was hanging over the top of the trailer. By the time Johnny could stop she had given a final convulsive wriggle and landed in the road.

Out we jumped and ran back, with some vague idea of catching her before she got away. We made a dive for her and missed, then looked up to see the second pig appear over the top of the parapet like a charging Amazon and scramble down into the road. They had torn a large hole in the wire and pushed back a corner of the tarpaulin. Both shot off at high speed, in the homeward direction, with Johnny and me panting after them.

Running like greyhounds, we managed to pass them and turn them back, only to see them shoot past the trailer and Jeep ahead of us. Several lorries and cars passed us and ignored our plight, and then some unsuspecting motorists stopped to watch the fun. Little did they dream what awaited them.

Johnny is a retiring fellow and invariably hesitates to put other people to any trouble. He will never ask a favour. I suspect that my whole family rather deplores a certain Gallic pushfulness in my make-up, which is known in France as having *du cran* and is appreciated. Anyway I pushed to good purpose, while he stood by undecided. In no time at all I had the occupants of the car out of their safe refuge and organised for action. They turned out to be three elegantly dressed gentlemen, with well-polished shoes and immaculately creased trousers.

Our best hope of success lay in trapping the pigs in the space between the bank and the side of the Jeep by blocking the exit at one end with a solid wedge of bodies while the others drove them into the trap. I persuaded my reluctant gang of pressed men to form this human wall, assuring them that all they had to do was to stand firm and the pigs wouldn't hurt them. They stood there, plugging the gap and looking slightly seasick, while Johnny and I doubled backwards and forwards until we had manoeuvred the pigs into position;

then we drove them into the narrow corridor, only to see my brave trio disintegrate like a pack of cards at their approach, jumping aside to let them pass.

There was nothing for it but for Johnny and me to form the barricade while our *aides-de-camp* did the corralling. This was eventually accomplished, in spite of the disruption caused by passing traffic, which frightened and scattered the pigs. By this time our helpers were no longer looking so well-groomed, I'm sorry to say.

We had the pigs cornered, but the worst was still to come. It was impossible for Johnny and me, unaided, to lift those heavy animals back into the trailer; it needed the joint effort of all present. Thus, before long, I was firmly grasping a sow's ear while one of our reluctant volunteers held the other one and his two friends gripped her tail. Johnny supported her belly.

'One, two, three, go!' he instructed. We all heaved, and in a trice the pig was in the trailer.

These tactics were successfully repeated with the second one, although the city suits of our Good Samaritans suffered considerably in the process. Johnny cleaned them up as best he could with an old sack and we were full of compunction and apologies. They took it extremely well.

On another occasion Johnny was taking two pigs to Taunton Market in the van. He glanced over his shoulder from time to time to see how they were faring, but they were model pigs, lying in the straw fast asleep.

Then, as he was chugging up a steep hill, he felt a jolt and looked back. The sharp incline had shifted the sleeping animals to the back of the van and their weight had forced open the door. He could see their bobbing rumps going hell for leather away from him down the hill. This time he had to retrieve them on his own and shut them in again. It was a Herculean task, but needless to say he managed it, since he has this special charisma of being able to accomplish unaided what others cannot achieve together.

Our son Peter still flinches when he recalls the time he was detailed to help his father round up absconding pigs. He had removed his sandals in order to follow a stampeding sow through the river and was running flat out, barefoot through the thistles, when he heard his father's shouts of encouragement from the opposite bank, 'Get in front of her, don't CHASE her. You'll never be any good at rugger if you can't turn a pig!'

I will never forget the awful day when Johnny asked me to help him ring some young pigs. This is sometimes done to pigs which are kept out of doors and consists of putting a metal clip in their nostrils to prevent them from rooting up grass and plants; it hurts when they try. These pigs were three or four months old and incredibly strong; they could wriggle and fight like mad. It is essential to hold the creature absolutely still, while the person who is doing the ringing carefully places the clips in position with a special instrument.

Johnny was going to do the ringing while I held the pigs, although it was obvious before we even started that I wouldn't be able to keep them under control. As soon as I picked one up and clasped my arms round it, it started to squirm and to shriek hysterically. Pigs scream almost before they are touched and their squeals are completely unnerving, quite apart from the trickiness of the job one is expected to perform. I begged Johnny to hold the pigs while I inserted the clips. Against his better judgement he agreed.

The result was that my first victim ducked its head as my trembling hand advanced and the clip fastened itself into its ear. Johnny told me to be more careful and I told him to hold its head steady. My next clip buried itself in its cheek and the third one clamped onto its lower lip. All this time it went on squealing, to the accompaniment of Johnny's imprecations and the chattering of my teeth and knocking of my knees. Johnny told me I was obviously quite incapable and he would have to do it while I held the pigs.

We changed places and I hung on grimly, but the pig jerked and squirmed and twisted in my arms, always reserving its major convulsion for the split second when he dived towards its snout with the clip. To my intense satisfaction his clips, like mine, flew all over its face. My joy was short-lived however, for he informed me that I was equally incapable of holding a pig and banished me from the shed, saying he could manage better on his own.

I retired from the battlefield in a rage and thought, 'Just let him try it!'

I should have known better. Twenty minutes later he walked in, quite unconcerned, and mentioned in passing that all the pigs were ringed.

CHAPTER 16

Casanova and Wild Galloways

I was nervous when I heard Johnny say we would have to buy our own bull, but fortunately all our bulls have been exceptionally docile and good natured. Arthur and Johnny have given them friendly slaps on their rumps when they wanted to move them, without them showing any signs of resentment. All have been Devons, which accounts for their good temper, together with the fact that for most of the year they run free with the cows.

Gradually I have overcome my fear, though I still keep a wary eye open. I have actually been bold enough to swoop down in the bull's path – under his very nose in fact – when he was only feet away and snatch up a sleeping lamb on which I feared he might tread. For me, this was quite a brave effort, because although country folk born and bred would think nothing of it, I was afraid. And there is no merit where there is no fear.

Once, soon after our first bull arrived, Johnny was out and Arthur came in to say that the bull had his horns entangled in the barbed wire strands which topped a fence designed to keep the cattle out of my chick-rearing pen. He said the bull must have been caught up for some time and was frantic and that he had tried to free him but couldn't manage it on his own.

I heard myself say, quite calmly, 'Well, Arthur, I shall have to come and give you a hand.'

I was anything but calm inside and really thought that I would be marching to my death. Then I remembered Victor Stevens at East Nethercote and, like a coward, went to ask him if he could help. To my relief, he agreed.

All the children were at home, and still quite young at the time, and it was a thrill for them as they peered from the safety of the hedge. I stood in the field, but within easy reach of cover, as we watched Victor and Arthur struggling to cut the wire from the horns of the maddened and terrified animal. Those men were heroes to us that day.

Finally, they released him and he shot away like a torpedo, mercifully not heading for us. There was still some wire twisted round his horns and he charged round the field, shaking and tossing his head, bellowing and leaping in the air. At last he shook it off and gradually quietened. The spectacle was at an end and the enthralled audience retreated indoors.

Every few years we have to change bulls to avoid them mating with their daughters. Our present bull is a proper Casanova. He is an unfaithful husband and has a roving eye which he turns on the wives of his neighbour, an aging bull entirely lacking in sex appeal, to judge by his harem's disloyalty. Our shameless fellow gets bored with his own wives and goes off in search of fresh friends and popsies new. No field will hold him. Johnny has strengthened all the gates and has been reluctantly forced to fix strands of barbed wire on top, a practice much to be deplored in hunting country, since it is dangerous for horses and hounds alike.

The bull's method of opening gates is to place his horns under one of the bars and lift it off its hinges. He then pushes it flat onto the ground and steps over it. In this way, flattening gate after gate, he reaches our neighbour's farm and pays his daily court to the fair damsels.

Regularly the phone rings and Johnny sets off to collect him. He is as sweet tempered as his predecessors and I am quite used to helping drive him back, though he doesn't really need any help; you just walk behind while the bull trots on ahead. Now and again he will make a quick turn and try to dodge back to the happy hunting grounds. The trick is to stand firm in his path, holding out your arms to make the barrier look a bit wider, then he meekly turns away again and continues on home. But this performance is an exasperating waste of time, hence the hated barbed wire which we have been forced to use.

Surprisingly our Casanova has never fought with his dispossessed rival so far as we know, for neither shows any battle scars.

Nethercote is a beef-rearing farm and we don't keep a dairy herd. Our cows are Devons or Devon crosses, plus a herd of Galloways whose offspring, if heifers, are served by the Devon bull. The Devons are tame and the Galloways wild, though not nearly as wild now as they were at first.

The system with beef rearing is to leave the calves with their mothers until they are about six months old, when they are separated from the cows so the latter can come into season again and bear another calf. By this time, the growing calves no longer need milk and can keep themselves on grass. In winter we bring the young stock into the cowsheds and feed them with hay or silage, but the older beasts winter in the open and are supplemented with hay once the grass becomes poor. Johnny drives round with bales of hay loaded into the back of the Jeep and the cows and bullocks come running when they hear the throb of the engine.

Often in February and March we have five or six weeks of biting east wind, which cuts back all the grass and seems to burn it like a searing flame. Then the hay is much in demand. However much we manage to make in the summer – very little sometimes when the weather is against us – we always wonder anxiously whether our supply will last the winter. This is one of Johnny's major worries, for hay is terribly expensive to buy and often almost unobtainable; yet there may be snow which covers the fields for days, or even weeks, when all the animals, including the sheep, have to have their daily ration.

From time to time our cattle have to be rounded up and driven, one at a time, into a small enclosure called a crush for their tuberculosis test, which is required by law. All herds now have to be attested at regular intervals and certified free from tuberculosis. The vet gives them an injection which shows a certain type of reaction if the animal is infected and comes back a few days later to inspect the results. This means the cattle have to be gathered and passed through the crush twice within a short space of time.

The crush is like a cage, made of strong metal or wooden bars, too narrow for the beast to turn round in and too high for it to jump over. The bullock is driven into the crush, which is closed at the front end. After the vet has injected it the front bars are raised to let it out. The trouble is driving the Galloways into it; being naturally wild and unapproachable they aren't easy to handle. The Devons and Devon crosses walk in quite meekly, but the Galloways plunge and rear and bolt madly around the cow yard, repeatedly swerving away from the entrance in spite of shouts and waving sticks. Fortunately they have no horns.

Once, some years ago when we weren't as well organised as we are now, we had all the cattle shut into the cow yard and I was helping the men drive them from the yard into a narrow passage in one of the cowsheds, which led directly to the crush. The stampede in the yard was terrific because the panicky Galloways were charging in all directions, bumping into each other and into the Devons who, in turn, were forced to join in the general mêlée.

The cobbled yard was slippery with dung and I was standing right in the middle of the turmoil when I lost my footing. In order not to fall to the ground and be trampled underfoot I grabbed the first thing to hand, which happened to be a Galloway. I hung on with both hands, managing somehow to hook one arm half-round its neck, but I was off my feet. The creature went careering off, dragging me with it and bumping me into the horns of the Devons.

I heard Johnny shouting, 'It's useless you trying to manhandle it into the cowshed! You'll never be able to handle a Galloway. Give it up, it's a waste of effort.'

Of course he had no idea I had lost my footing, and even in my plight I felt a glow of pride that he had imagined I would have the temerity to try my strength with one of those devils. I felt like a cow-puncher at a rodeo, and as I managed just then to regain my feet I kept the truth to myself.

On another of those TB testing occasions I had an even more dramatic encounter with a Galloway.

All available help had been enlisted. Gillian was stationed

outside the crush, writing down the number of the earmark of each beast and its age. Arthur was working the crush and assisting the vet, while I was in the cow yard, helping Johnny drive the cattle into the cowshed, through the narrow passage between the calf pens and into the cattle crush. Some of them were extremely reluctant to move from the end of the passage into the crush and we had to whack them with sticks and twist their tails to urge them forward.

One old Galloway defied all our efforts and was holding up the beasts behind her. Finally we manoeuvred her into the calf pen on the left, which was divided from the passage by a high concrete wall. We closed the door on her and the vet injected her in there, with Johnny and Arthur hanging on to her. She was now quiet, so we left her in the pen while we got on with driving the others through, urging on a file of about five beasts, with another Galloway bringing up the rear.

As I stepped forward to give the last one a whack on the rump Johnny shouted, 'Look out, she kicks!'

I checked in mid-stride and her kick whistled past my leg within an inch of me and hit a heavy gate with a crack like a pistol shot, knocking it over. On top of this, the passage between the calf pens had become completely blocked because the foremost beast refused to budge.

Johnny and I were behind the press of cattle, separated from the front by the throng of backs and flanks, and couldn't reach the recalcitrant cow to urge her on. As I was near the adjoining calf pen, I nipped in through the door so I could lean over the wall and hit her with my stick.

Having duly thwacked her, losing my stick in the process, I was unconcernedly returning through the pen when the Galloway we had incarcerated there put her head down and charged me. I was taken completely by surprise and pinned against the back wall. She then proceeded, without giving me room to escape, to butt me repeatedly with her lowered head, pounding away at my thigh.

Johnny couldn't reach the calf pen because of the press of cattle in the passage. As he forced his way through them, he shouted, 'Get out!'

'I can't get out!' I yelled back, and I was really frightened.

Even if I could have moved from where my attacker had me pinned I could never have hoisted myself over the high wall, nor had time to unbolt the door. I thought she was going to kill me. Thank God Johnny managed to push through the cows and reach the wall of the pen. Leaning over, he belaboured the Galloway on the nose with his stick, driving her back after repeated blows. Then he unbolted the door and I escaped.

My thigh developed a bruise the size of a plate; black, blue, purple and red, with bumps on it like hens' eggs.

'She's the old girl who always charges you when she has a calf,' Johnny remarked to me afterwards.

But he hadn't expected it as she had no calf at that time. I think the cow was frightened by our efforts to get her into the crush, followed by further alarm while she was held in the pen and injected, and when she saw me there she thought, 'This is too much. They're going to do some other nasty thing to me and I won't stand for it.'

CHAPTER 17

I sat in the icy river

One day Arthur came down from the top of Bye Common, a hill nearby on which we had grazing rights, to say that one of our Galloways was in trouble calving; she was walking about with the calf's head sticking out behind. This was really serious and she would need immediate help. Johnny and Arthur went up there to drive her down. She charged at them on sight and Arthur only just jumped out of the way. She charged him twice more on the way down.

Somehow they manoeuvred her into the crush, but when they examined her it was immediately obvious that this was a job for the vet. It was an enormous dead calf. When the vet arrived he gave her an injection to make her dopey. Then all hands were summoned, including mine.

Nothing could be done while the cow stood upright in the crush, she had to be turned on her back. This required a big effort from us all, dazed and quiet as she had become, because she was heavy. In addition, the crush was so narrow that her legs got mixed up with the bars as we pulled and strained to turn her, first onto her side and then onto her back. The calf was huge and so firmly wedged that we couldn't budge it, although we all heaved on ropes. Johnny had to rig up a pulley. In the end it came away and we dragged the cow out and into a stall in the cowshed.

We knew it would be impossible to get near her once she had recovered and that there would be no question of being able to milk her. The only thing we could do was to try to make her accept another calf, so Johnny asked a dealer to get him a black one from market. He left the dead one with her, to stimulate her maternal instincts, but she was feeling rotten and didn't take much notice of it.

By the time the new calf arrived the cow was better. She had never before been confined and was restive; nobody could get into the stall. Johnny opened the door wide enough to pull out the dead calf and pushed in the little stranger, while he and Arthur stood by to rescue it if necessary. She wasn't vicious with it, she just ignored it. It stood cowering in one corner, lost, bewildered and wanting its own mother.

It made no attempt at all to go up to her and suck, yet we knew it must be hungry. We felt if only the calf would take some notice of the cow, she would accept it; she must have been feeling uncomfortable and longing for her udder to be relieved. But she made no overtures to it and they continued to stand at opposite ends of the stall, both looking miserable.

What a time Arthur had with that calf. He and Johnny hoped Nature would have her way and it would suck once it felt really famished. They were determined not to feed it. Hours went by and turned into days and still the *status quo* remained. Arthur spent every spare moment leaning over the wall with a long pole, patiently pushing the calf to get it into position beneath the cow's udder, but it seemed to have no idea at all what was expected of it. Often, no sooner had he at last manoeuvred it into position than the cow moved away. She wasn't hostile and would sniff it at times, but she didn't moo to it.

After a couple of days we were all growing anxious about the calf and wondered how long it would be safe to persevere. Every time Arthur came into the kitchen I asked for news. I had nightmares in which it was found dead in the morning.

Early on the third day I could bear it no longer and warmed up a bucket of milk. Johnny was out on the farm, so I carried it to the cowshed, where I found Arthur engaged as usual in prodding the calf gently towards the cow. He opened the door slightly and pulled it out. Then, while I held the bucket under its nose, he dipped his hand in the warm milk, with his wrist held downwards and three bunched fingers poking upwards, so the calf would suck them and drink in the milk at the same time. Gently he pushed its head down towards the milk, and to my joy it started to suck.

Arthur was encouraging it, with the same devotion he showed to all the calves in his care, 'Now come on my little man. Have another little drop. That's better. There's a good little man!'

When he thought the calf had had enough he pushed it back into the stall. We then witnessed a miracle. It dived straight under the mother and began to suck her, while she stood there quietly, looking blissful as her full udder was eased. Our troubles were over. What glad tidings for Johnny when he came in.

Arthur was a wonderful worker and couldn't bear to be idle. He enjoyed his work and after a day on the farm would toil in the garden until it was too dark to see, nothing we could say would stop him. To our great sorrow he eventually left us. After 60-odd years of cautious bachelorhood he suddenly announced to Johnny that he wished to return to Surrey to be married. Johnny observed him carefully to make sure he was all right, but he appeared to be normal, though naturally somewhat nervous at having to reveal his defection to one who had so often congratulated him on escaping the pitfall of matrimony. No baleful warnings would shake him and we sadly had to let him go.

Johnny wasn't entirely without help when Arthur left so unexpectedly, for Tom Gage had been with us for three years. Tom had come to us to learn about sheep farming on Exmoor, with a view to acquiring a farm of his own in our neighbourhood. He fitted into our household and into the West Country community as a whole as if he had been born and bred to it, became enormously popular with everyone and gradually made himself indispensable to Johnny.

Tom and I shared another adventure in connection with a calving cow. Johnny had gone to Dulverton in the Jeep and Tom was riding round the sheep on his mare, Rosie, when a man came to deliver something with a lorry. He told me that a cow was calving in the river and that she'd almost had it.

I thought he meant that the calf was almost born, so I jumped into Tom's Landrover, taking the man with me, for I feared the cow might drop the calf into the river and it would drown. I thought we might be able to drive her out of the water up onto the bank if we could reach her in time. But I found what he had meant was that the cow herself had nearly had it and was in danger of drowning. She was lying exhausted on the rocky river bed with the water flowing over her. We could glimpse the submerged head of her partly-born calf.

The man and I scrambled down the bank into the river and tried to persuade the cow to get up, but she couldn't. She knew it and made no attempt to help herself. She had scraped the skin off both knees and had worn herself out in her struggles, and in her efforts to calve. Now, indeed, she was at the point of no return and could hardly hold her head above water.

I realised I should have to find Tom and heaven knew where he was, so I left the man supporting the cow's head and flew back to the house. There I grabbed our hunting horn and blew several mighty blasts, like Roland at Ronceval blowing his horn with bursting lungs for Charlemagne, so far away. Compared with Johnny's, mine were pretty feeble efforts really, but like Charlemagne, Tom heard the SOS from afar and came cantering down into the valley, to pick up the message I had left for him. He then rode on along the lane, to find me sitting in the river with the cow's head on my knees.

Our friend in need, the lorry driver, gave us a hand in our efforts to get her up. We all pulled together, trying to get some purchase on her, yanking at her tail and attempting to straighten her legs, but she was beyond helping herself and we could do nothing. The driver had to go, for he was late on his rounds, but gave us a rope from his lorry. It was obvious we would have to use it and we were wondering hopelessly how to set about it when Johnny drew up beside us in the Jeep.

He and Tom struggled to extricate that poor cow for the next couple of hours, before they at last succeeded. During most of that time I sat in the icy river, keeping her head above water. As soon as I released it for a second, which I was sometimes forced to do in order to shift my position among the slippery rocks, her head flopped under.

First Johnny had to get the dead calf away, which he

managed to do while the cow was still in the river. Then, with much manoeuvring, they slid an old door under her and lashed it to another door, tilted up the side of the bank. Finally, they tied a rope round the top part of her body and under her front legs.

The lane is bordered by the river on one side and a steep hillside on the other, with not enough space to allow a straight pull up the bank. So Johnny decided they would have to use both vehicles. He stationed the Jeep opposite the spot where the cow lay and ran the rope from her round its back axle and on to Tom's Landrover. Tom then drove the Landrover slowly forward along the lane, with the Jeep acting as a winch. Countless times the cow's limp body slid back off the door and the whole process had to be repeated, or the door became embedded in the bank. In the end they got her out and onto a gate, which they towed slowly back to the farm.

Soon she was safe and sound in a stall, warmly surrounded by straw. She made a rapid recovery and we bought her another calf, which she welcomed gladly.

Some time after that Johnny found a sick calf up over. He brought it down and put it in one of the stables before phoning the vet to ask him to have a look at it. Then, as he had to go out, he left me in charge. The vet duly arrived and made his diagnosis and we returned together to the kitchen, where he gave me two bottles, each containing a clear yellow liquid. He warmed one of the bottles in hot water and told me to give the calf half the bottle at once and the remaining half later. As for the second bottle, he had just given it a tablespoonful and another tablespoonful should be given in four hours.

I saw him out to his car and came back for the warm bottle. I put out my hand to feel which bottle had been warmed; the first one on which it fell was standing on the corner of the Rayburn. It was warm, so I took it to the stable and poured half of it down the calf's throat. As I walked back I glanced idly at the label and felt a surge of panic when I read, 'One tablespoon at four hourly intervals'. I rushed in and felt the other bottle, standing on the kitchen table, but I knew what I would find – it was the one the vet had warmed. The Rayburn had warmed the other. I was paralysed with shock, sure I had killed the calf.

It was some moments before I could get my mind to function. I knew it was no good phoning the vet for advice as he had told me he had a long list of calls to make, and Johnny wouldn't be home for hours. I had no idea what to do to make the calf sick, or even whether they could be sick. I knew horses couldn't. Besides, I might merely make matters worse.

Having given the poor creature the wrong medicine, I no longer dared to give it the half from the correct bottle, for it might be bad to give it one on top of the other. I simply waited for Johnny and did nothing, in a state of indecision and dread. I felt criminally careless and I trembled to think what he would say.

The hours went by very slowly and I paid constant visits to the stable, expecting each time to find the calf in its death throes. But it seemed no worse. Finally I heard the Jeep and went out to meet Johnny.

As he came towards me I said, 'I've done a terrible thing,' and burst into tears.

At once he put a comforting arm around me and I blurted

out my story. Of course he was very understanding and told me not to worry at all, that the wrong medicine had probably done no harm and that, even if it had, he thought the calf was going to die anyway. It did in fact eventually die, but it was about a week later. Thankfully, I don't think I was to blame. Johnny never uttered a word of criticism. He said it could have happened to anyone.

CHAPTER 18

'The Circus'

For years, we had too many horses on the farm and I never heard the last of it from Johnny.

When we were living in Surrey, there were riding stables right opposite Parley Brook House and the three younger children had lessons. Peter, the eldest, missed them through being at boarding school. They loved riding and their dream, like that of all children who live in the country, was to have ponies of their own. We couldn't possibly keep one in our small paddock, which was given over to pigs and poultry, but we promised rashly that if ever we had a farm we would see what we could do. The farm was very much a pipe dream at that time; once it became a reality the children immediately brought up the subject again. We decided we'd give them ponies for Christmas and began to make inquiries.

Johnny was in this plan with me up to the hilt, whatever he may have said later, and was a party to the whole affair, though I must admit that I was the chief instigator. I was aided and abetted in this by our land girl, B. She was a splendid horsewoman and knew all there was to know about teaching children to ride and to look after their ponies.

It was Johnny, in fact, who made the first inquiries and it was he who went to Dulverton to inspect Chips, who became

Hilary's pony. But later on, when the ponies misbehaved, he kept up the continual refrain, 'You insisted on having them. I was against it from the start.'

B went with me to give her verdict on the ponies for the others. We chose Bracken for Stanley and Muffet, a pretty little Dartmoor, for Gillian. Peter had none. He wasn't keen to ride and later we gave him a motorcycle to compensate. In addition to the children's ponies, Johnny had a heavy hunter, Ranger, B had brought with her her beautiful Arab gelding, Kismet, and we had a small carthorse, Peter, whom we had inherited with the farm.

Thus we started with six horses and it wasn't long before Hilary had saved up birthday and Christmas money and bought herself a six month old foal, Titbits, which she wished to break in herself. On top of that our neighbour's Exmoor stallion crossed the river to visit our mares and Muffet was soon in foal.

The situation rapidly became impossible. Hilary's Chips was the ringleader, ably seconded by Muffet, the Dartmoor pony. Chips could open any gate on the farm, breaking down those which he couldn't unlatch or unhinge, and Muffet had no need of gates for she could jump up the steepest bank and force her way through the thickest hedge. Where Chips or Muffet led, the rest of the herd would follow. They found their way into Johnny's newly seeded grass and what they didn't eat they churned up with their hooves as they galloped round and round, in an excess of high spirits.

As soon as one gap was filled in, Muffet made another, and wherever the ponies went, the sheep weren't far behind, breaking into the turnips and kale, which Johnny was saving for the bad weather, and the grass he was keeping in reserve for lambing time.

Ranger and Kismet were kept in during the winter, so they were blameless, but the others had to winter out. The children were all at boarding school, of one sort or another, which meant that the ponies were only ridden during the holidays and ran wild for a large part of the year. Frequently the hunt came through the farm, either the staghounds or the foxhounds, and at times the riders left the gates open. Our entire herd would set off in pursuit, with manes streaming and hooves pounding, and end up on someone else's farm, whence they had to be rounded up and brought back. No wonder Johnny nearly went mad.

I was his whipping boy and received the brunt of his exasperation.

Almost daily I heard how we were being ruined by the ponies, how we might as well give up farming and turn the place into a circus. He would rumble on, saying I had always spoilt the children. Didn't I know that one horse ate as much as 15 sheep, quite apart from what they ruined? We weren't landed gentry, we were working farmers and it was time I realised it. I was responsible for buying the ponies and now I had better get rid of them. No farm could be made to pay if it was overrun by horses.

All this made sense of course. Johnny's annoyance was justified and something clearly had to be done, but he did nothing himself, except grumble and wear me down. I felt depressed and helpless.

The crisis came one morning, when he and I set off on a tour of the sheep at the beginning of lambing. We had a flock of in-lamb ewes, very near their time, in our field called Pullwater. Just as we had nearly reached them, the entire herd of ponies broke through the hedge and galloped straight into the middle of the flock, leaping, prancing and kicking up their heels. The ewes were too heavy to get out of the way of the flying hooves and many got kicked. Two were killed outright, both carrying twins, others were injured and some later aborted, bearing dead lambs.

Johnny was in a tremendous rage as we ran about, trying to drive the ponies away from the sheep. When he had driven them off and was examining the casualties he told me he was coming straight down to the house to ring up the knackers and tell them to come to fetch all the ponies that very day. I knew he really meant it. But first he had to find the ponies, which had disappeared, and shut them in somewhere to prevent it happening again. So I had a short interval at my disposal before he could reach the telephone.

I left him waving both fists at the sky and could hear his curses as I ran down the hill. I grabbed the telephone directory and rang every dealer I could find and everyone else I could think of who might know of someone wanting a pony. By the time Johnny arrived I had put Bracken in the hands of a dealer, dictated over the phone our advertisement for the sale of Muffet's foal and Hilary's colt, and agreed to sell Muffet herself, a registered Dartmoor, as a beach pony for £20, the best price I could get in such an emergency. Anything was better than the knackers.

We were allowed to keep Chips. Johnny relented about him since he could no longer be the ringleader once he had no ring to lead. Chips continued his naughty habits, opening gates and breaking out of any enclosure, but since his only companion was Peter the carthorse he became less venturesome.

Johnny had Ranger trained as a showjumper and sold him.

Then he bought Sunshine, a heavyweight hunter. She is a light chestnut with a dark chestnut mane and tail, 15.2 hands high, and was nine years old when she joined the family. She arrived on Thursday, 7 February 1957 and consequently Johnny had a very busy day.

Arthur came into the kitchen the following morning and remarked, 'The Governor promised to help me yesterday to shift the cows round in the cowsheds. It must have gone out of his mind.'

Everything went out of his mind, I think, except the one word 'Sunshine', which flooded it all day with warmth and brightness.

Sunshine's coat had been completely clipped out and she had to remain in, apart from daily exercise, except on a fine warm day. After ushering her into her new quarters, Johnny spent the rest of the day going backwards and forwards between the stable, the kitchen and the barn, his 'the stock won't last the winter' expression replaced by a happy smile. All my buckets were whisked away, and in the end even the heavy cast iron cauldron in which I boil the hams was carried off, so that she could have a utensil for her water which couldn't be knocked over.

Johnny gave her a large wooden box brimming with oats, but she didn't seem to fancy them, so off he went to get some from a different bin because he thought the mice might have been at the first lot and put her off. She did him the honour of accepting the second offering. He then fetched a haynet and filled it with hay for her, but as she showed no interest in it he took it out again and replaced it with some of his best green meadow hay, which she kindly deigned to eat.

The next thing he did was to take off her two rugs, admire

her and inspect her from all angles and then put them back on again. When I teased him about this he said, 'You always have to take their rugs off once a day to air them,' though I'm not sure whether 'them' meant rugs or horses.

He pottered about for hours in the barn, trying to find two stirrups that matched, sorting out all the tack, muttering about what the children had done with it, and cleaning his saddle and oiling his bridle. Then he came in and found my best white enamel bucket, which I thought I had successfully hidden, and prepared some hot mash. Last thing at night, he was still trundling back and forth with more buckets of water and fresh supplies of hay and was surprised when she wasn't hungry.

The following morning he rode off to see the sheep.

When he returned from his round he exclaimed, 'Sunshine is a wonderful horse! She goes uphill with a sprightly step, whereas I really had to push old Ranger. She has plenty of spirit; she wants to be on the go all the time and I had to restrain her. But she stands perfectly still for me to mount her and she's wonderful at opening gates, even the most difficult ones. I shall breed from her and she will have a lovely foal.'

Tommie and I burst out laughing, because his first thought is always to breed from his new acquisitions.

Sunshine did indeed produce some lovely foals and she has now been joined by her son Shindy and daughter Serena. We also have another brood mare, Benny, with her foal. Yet, curiously, I am no longer asked if I realise that one horse eats as much as 15 sheep.

When Shindy was on the way Johnny would hopefully measure Sunshine amidships every week, to make sure she was beginning to swell, but as he usually mislaid the tobacco tin on which he had scratched the previous week's measurement he wasn't much wiser.

Excitement mounted as the day of the confinement drew closer and the 11 months of waiting came to an end. Johnny decided to keep her in the stable for the event. A couple of days beforehand he carried over a mattress and some blankets and made himself a bed in her manger. After spending a somewhat uncomfortable first night, he made up a proper bed in the adjoining stall. In the middle of the night he heard a plop, and when he shone his torch over the wall he discovered Sunshine happily licking her son, who was struggling to get up.

Shindy was 'the prettiest little foal' that Johnny, or any of us for that matter, had ever seen and his delighted owner was happily convinced that one day he would be 'worth at least £600.'

CHAPTER 19

George and Whissups

George was another high-spirited acquisition, a bay hunter who definitely had breeding, though we were unable to trace his pedigree. Johnny bought him knowing very little about him, but he liked the look of him and said he had a kind eye. He thought George might have the makings of a point-to-pointer. Our part of the world is grand point-to-point country and the races, held in the spring on various beautifully situated courses, are a major attraction and a pretext for all farmers to take the day off. They are organised by the various hunts in our neighbourhood, to supplement their funds.

Eagerly Johnny embarked on the early stages of George's training and found, to his joy, that he could jump and had a good turn of speed. He engaged a 15 year old girl, Jane-Anne, a splendid little rider, to exercise him daily and train him over jumps.

My good double saucepan, of course, was commandeered for George's brews of linseed and my only small heavy aluminium saucepan for a barley brew. Both these concoctions had to be kept continually simmering on the Rayburn, with water being added periodically as it evaporated. Woe betide the hapless individual – usually me – who allowed the pans to boil dry, or removed one from the hot plate in order to proceed with normal cooking activities and subsequently forgot to replace it.

As winter turned to spring George was duly entered for three point-to-points and the time came when the first one was only a few days away. An experienced jockey agreed to ride him and amid mounting excitement Jane-Anne, who was too young to ride him on the great day, continued to put him through his paces. Every afternoon she took him out for a couple of hours. It was primrose time, and one fateful afternoon I asked her to bring me back a bunch, to post to my sister in London. This request was probably responsible in part for the disaster which followed; you *do not* pick primroses when exercising a race horse.

Jane-Anne was riding George home when she came to the cattle grid on our boundary, half-way up the lane from Larcombe Foot. On the left of the grid is the gate and she dismounted to open it, holding the bridle in her right hand and the primroses in the other.

I was in the kitchen that afternoon when the door from the yard burst open and Jane-Anne stumbled in, sobbing uncontrollably. Fear shot through me, even before I could understand a single word over which she was choking.

'George!' she gasped, 'George!'

'What's happened?' I asked.

She was so shaken with sobs I could gather nothing. Finally I made out that George had caught his leg in the cattle grid.

'Is it broken?'

'No, I don't think so.'

'Is he still there?'

She was weeping hysterically, and shaking with shock, but I understood her to gasp out, 'Yes.'

Instantly I flew upstairs and told Johnny, who was in the bathroom. Both of us rushed downstairs and through the kitchen into the yard and jumped into the Jeep – Jane-Anne had vanished. We drove at top speed to the cattle grid, through the rain-filled potholes. As soon as we could see it in the distance we saw at once that the horse wasn't there. But there was a dark lump on the ground near it, which we both thought was George, and we both knew he must have broken a leg in his struggles to free himself.

'Oh my God, my lovely horse!' cried Johnny.

As we drew nearer the grid we saw that the lump was actually a bush, not George, but still we knew he must have maimed himself in struggling free. Frantically we glanced to right and left, looking for him and dreading what we would see.

I was still scanning both sides of the road beyond the grid as we drew up to it when suddenly Johnny called out in a strangled voice, 'Oh no! Look! Oh my lovely horse. Darling, I can't bear it.'

I hardly dared look and had to force myself to follow his eyes. He was gazing straight ahead with an expression of the utmost horror and still I could see nothing.

'Look at the *road*,' he groaned.

And then I saw it. An enormous pool of blood in the middle of the road, just beyond the grid. Near the gate lay the scattered primroses.

Stunned with shock, we crossed the grid and searched for poor George, the whole situation made more sinister by the fact that he was missing. We pictured him dragging himself away in agony and ran to the river bank to see if he had gone to water. We tried to follow the blood spoor, but could find no trail leading away from the bloody pool in the road. We tried in all directions and all the time we thought of George in pain, trailing a broken leg.

'We must find him,' Johnny kept repeating.

'You'll have to go back for your gun,' I said, 'I'm afraid you're going to need it.'

'Yes, but we must find him first,' he said.

We drove down to the main road, found no blood stains anywhere and in desperation returned to the cattle grid, to find Jane-Anne running towards us from the direction of the house. Breathlessly she told us George was at home in the stable and that he was badly cut but with no leg broken.

Somehow there had been a misunderstanding about George still being caught in the cattle grid. What had happened was that while Jane-Anne was trying to unlatch the gate he must have pawed the ground and his foreleg slipped between the first and second bars of the grid. Jane-Anne hung on to the bridle while he threw himself about. In his struggles, he got a hind leg caught as well and in fact, Jane-Anne thought, at one time he had both hind legs gripped by the lacerating metal bars. He reared and plunged, freeing first one leg and then another, until at last he staggered away from the trap on three legs, holding up a hind leg.

For about ten minutes, he stood shuddering in a pool in the road, while the blood ran from his wounds into the water. Gradually the large shallow puddle turned crimson, and of course, when we came upon it, we didn't know that much of it was rain water.

When George was able to put his foot lightly to the ground, Jane-Anne led him through the gate and he hobbled home, so the trail of blood led away on the opposite side of the grid from where we had been searching. After blurting out the news to me in the kitchen, she had gone to the stable to put a rug on him. Then she heard us go off in the Jeep and had run after us.

George was badly wounded and for months afterwards we feared he might never again be sound. In the end he recovered completely and did quite promisingly in his first few point-to-points a year later. Then he dropped dead just after passing the post at the end of his fourth race. It was a tragedy for us all, particularly for Johnny. He looked so stricken. The autopsy showed an enlarged heart, which only an x-ray could have revealed.

After Gillian's pony Muffet, the Dartmoor, had been so unceremoniously bundled off to the beach, and sufficient time had elapsed for Johnny to forget about his allergy to ponies, he bought her a lovely little grey mare called Whissups. She was the heroine of a remarkable acrobatic feat which was the crowning episode in a hectic morning at Nethercote.

It was lambing time again and we were all rushed off our feet. In addition, we had two appointments that morning, to complicate the remorseless timetable. One was with an official from the Ministry of Agriculture, who was expected at 10.45 to inspect a bull calf, which we hoped he would pass for breeding purposes. We had bred him from a Devon bull and a black Galloway cow and he had turned out to be a perfect replica of a red Devon, but without horns, a result which is difficult to obtain and much sought after. In fact well-known breeding establishments were concentrating their resources on producing polled Devons. We were proud of our little fellow and had visions of using him to sire our own herd.

Our other appointment was with some people who were coming to see Whissups with a view to buying her for their daughter. We had decided to sell her because by then Gillian was away for eight months of the year at Cheltenham, my old school. So Whissups had been brought in and groomed and was awaiting her visitors in a stall in the stables. In the next stall was Sunshine, who can open any stable door unless the bolt is pushed right home and the catch turned firmly down.

The day started badly because Johnny went up over before breakfast on his lambing inspection and found that a young ewe, having dropped her lamb, had run off and left it. He found the erring mother, but was unable to catch her, so he went up again with Tom immediately after breakfast.

At 10.15 our dogs barked and Gillian, convinced the people were arriving to see Whissups, made off rapidly into the meadows because she was nervous of being asked to show off the pony's paces in front of some highly-skilled and critical girl rider. I had to interrupt my lamb bottle-feeding round to greet the visitors. But the car which drew up in the yard contained our man from the Ministry, half an hour early by Johnny's reckoning; dead on time by his own. He was annoyed to be kept waiting because he had another appointment, but nothing would have induced me to show him the bull calf, since I might have said the wrong thing. As I kept him talking his face grew longer and his temper shorter.

Meanwhile Gillian, hiding in the meadows, had found a ewe trying in vain to lamb and needing urgent help. So she hurried back and made for the stables, hoping to find Johnny and Tom. She looked over the stable door, to discover that Sunshine had opened the connecting door between the two stalls and was standing where Whissups had been.

At first Gillian couldn't see Whissups, so she craned her neck to see if she was behind Sunshine. At the back of the stall, running the length of the rear wall, is a concrete manger about two feet high and topped off by a stout steel bar. Lying on her back in the manger was Whissups, unable to move, with three legs sticking up in the air and the fourth leg trapped in the narrow gap between the manger and bar.

Fortunately, at that moment Johnny and Tom arrived. The poor cattle expert was forgotten in the excitement, since it was imperative to release Whissups before she broke her leg. But he came up trumps, forgot his next appointment and offered to help.

Tom had to sit on the pony's head to prevent her from struggling, while Johnny filed through the steel bar, each end of which was embedded in concrete. Once the leg was free we all had to heave to get her out of the manger, where she was firmly wedged. She was a heavy weight to shift. When finally we got her right way up she was little the worse for her exploit, though she had skinned her leg in various places. She certainly wasn't fit to be displayed to prospective buyers. Luckily they telephoned to say they had bought another pony.

Then Johnny hurried off to deliver the lamb in the meadow and the man from the Ministry inspected the little bull on his own. Alas, our hopes were dashed, for he wouldn't pass him and we were forced to have our golden calf castrated.

CHAPTER 20

The Hunt and Haymaking

After a few years we bought Room Hill, 128 acres of land on the other side of the Exe from our Brakes. Flat topped, it is covered with bracken and heather and makes excellent summer grazing for the flock of Cheviots which has now increased our stock of sheep.

Room Hill has a frontage onto the Exford-Dulverton road, bounded by a hedge, and is accessible to the road by two gateways. Originally there was only a narrow path up the steep face of the hill, but Johnny has made a proper track by going up and down with the Jeep. From the top, there is a magnificent view of the countryside for miles around and the whole farm is spread out before your eyes on the opposite side of the river like a map. We can stand up there and gaze across, checking the whereabouts of sheep, bullocks and horses.

For riding enthusiasts, there is a good level gallop for some distance along the top of the hill. Riders to hounds know it well and we have often stood on the Brakes to watch the proceedings. We have seen the hunt on the top of Room Hill, horses and riders silhouetted against the skyline while they checked, and we have watched the hunted stag moving silently through the bracken on the hillside beneath them, making his way down to the river. I have held my breath and kept my fingers crossed for the graceful creature, praying that he would get well away before hounds picked up his scent.

I know, as do all other farmers in our part of the country, that the deer do a considerable amount of damage to crops, not only by what they eat, but by what they waste. They will uproot turnips, take one bite out of them and leave them lying in the field, to be spoiled by frost. We have had an entire crop ruined in this way. It is clear that the deer have to be kept away from the farms and their number restricted.

Nonetheless, illogically perhaps, we love to know that some of them find shelter in the valley and it is always a pleasure to come upon a couple of hinds and their calves, quietly grazing, as you drive down to the end of the lane to post a letter. Often we have stood in our garden, or at a bedroom window, and followed the leisurely progress of a stag and hinds through the bracken and bushes across the river.

Thus it is with trepidation that we watch the hounds come pouring down the face of Room Hill, following the line of the deer with noses to the ground and giving tongue, while the riders gallop along the brow in search of a gentler incline for their descent. Although I recognise the undoubted necessity for reducing the numbers of both deer and foxes, and that other methods of destruction are either impracticable in our area or more cruel than hunting, it is nonetheless saddening to see, at the end of a successful hunt, a magnificent stag roped onto the back of a car, his proud antlers erect no more.

Yet it is impossible, even as a mere onlooker, not to feel the excitement of the hunt, not to respond to its pageantry. There is a thrill in the sound of the horn, the chorus of hounds in full cry, the flash of pink coats in the sunlight, the sight of the riders streaming past on their beautiful hunters. Whatever one's view on the ethics of hunting, it would be difficult not to be stirred by its panoply.

A day out with hounds is the breath of life to most Exmoor farmers. Hunting is their chief relaxation. If it is abolished it will be a sad day for them, for it is part of the fabric of their lives.

Gatherings of the farming community are unfortunately becoming fewer, now that farming has become more streamlined and less manual labour is needed.

When we first came to Nethercote, hay-making was a neighbourly concern. We used to turn the hay with pitchforks then, and rake it into rows with long wooden rakes, all the family helping. I had to take off my wedding ring in the hay field because the constant handling of fork or rake blistered the base of my finger.

Once the hay was ready to be carried, Johnny would attach a sweep to the front of the tractor. This had long wooden prongs, like fingers, which slid under each mound of hay, sweeping it off the ground. When it was fully loaded, the tractor was driven to the rising hayrick and then reversed so that the prongs slid backwards, leaving their pile of hay by the rick.

The men made the rick, while the children and I took turns at the tractor. The children drove it from the moment they were tall enough to reach the combined clutch and brake – around 13 years old. It was only possible to use the sweep in the more level fields. On the steeper slopes, we pitched the hay by hand into a trailer drawn by the tractor, and into a cart to which Peter, the carthorse, was harnessed.

As a rule, two people pitched and a third stood on top of the load to receive the forkfuls and arrange them so it was well balanced. Then off would trundle tractor or horse across the field to the rick, with most of us perched precariously on top to keep it in place on the steep incline. The trailer would often be tilted at a perilous angle, and many a time part of the load with its human anchors has cascaded down onto the hard ground, amid shrieks of merriment.

The trailer would be drawn up alongside the rick and unloaded, with the more experienced members of the party on top of the rick to fashion it. This is quite an expert job, for it has to be squared up and constructed sufficiently solidly to withstand the winter gales.

Haymaking is always a cheerful time, providing the weather is good and we are free from the pall of gloom which hangs over us when it rains continually and the hay is rotting on the ground because it is too wet to carry. You are generally working against time, desperately trying to get the last load in before it rains. I load thermoses and sandwiches into baskets and take them out to the haymakers and we snatch a few moments for tea in between loads. Work goes on until the evening dew makes the hay too damp.

We have our own hay baler now, and also a special attachment to the tractor for turning the swathes; but we still have to do some of the work by hand on our steepest ground.

In the old days, farmers would provide tractors and trailers and as much manpower as could be spared, going from one neighbour's farm to the next. Great was the merrymaking after the day's work was done, when the haymakers would gather in the big farm kitchen, with its open hearth and hams hanging from hooks in the beams. They would consume with relish home cured ham and mounds of freshly baked bread, cakes and scones which the womenfolk had prepared, quaff pints of cider and home brewed ale, and sing folk songs far into the night.

The coming of mechanisation, which has made farms largely self-sufficient, although a boon in many ways, has killed for ever the inter-dependence of the farming community, and with it much of the good fellowship and sense of comradeship which resulted. Rarer are the opportunities now for those cheerful gatherings of neighbours, except by deliberate invitation, and such parties lack the spirit of companionship which a day's hard work together in the fields engenders.

It is difficult to convey to anyone who hasn't sampled it the deep satisfaction of work in the hay fields. It is compounded of many things. There is the feeling of well-being produced by hard muscular work in the open air, the companionship of fellow toilers, the pleasure of knowing you are helping to secure the winter's keep for the stock.

Above all, it is work normally carried out in the sunshine of a summer day. You breathe in the lovely fragrance of the hay, you watch the shadows lengthening, the play of light and shade on the hills, and you hear the country sounds around you: the distant whirring of some other farmer's mower, the shouted command of a shepherd to his dog across the valley, a pony's whinny or the crowing of a cock. Perhaps the cuckoo will be calling from the trees across the river, if you are fortunate enough to be getting your hay in before he has flown. Whenever I hear him I think how lucky I am to live in the country.

CHAPTER 21

Where are the sprouts?

We long ago decided in principle that it is more economical to keep hens in deep litter than let them have free range, at least as far as we are concerned at Nethercote, since they lay in the thick hedges where we never find the eggs. In practice this doesn't always work out, because as soon as the sun shines after the dismal winter we feel sorry for them and think how nice it would be for them to be outside in the sun and the fresh grass.

So we open the door and out they fly happily, to hide their nests where only the dogs can find them and to roost at night in Johnny's implement shed, decorating the tractor and the rotavator with their droppings. This annoys him intensely and I am asked why on earth I let them out, when in fact it was he who had weakly opened the door.

Thus it came about, one fateful night, that a fox crept up on some of them who had selected too low a perch. Foxes don't just carry away what they need for food, they cause real carnage; biting off the heads of their victims and then making off with one, perhaps coming back for another, and leaving the other corpses strewn around. The next morning we found four headless hens and only Hilary was at home to help us eat them, and her godfather, Uncle Mumpti, who was staying with us.

Now it happened that I had been reading the Farmer and Stockbreeder in the bathroom. The 'Women's Page', written by the more leisurely farmers' wives for the benefit of their less well-organised sisters, informed me that you could make a tough old boiler taste like the tenderest of young broilers by Mrs So-and-So's special method. I only vaguely remember the procedure, but I believe you had to marinate the bird for 12 hours in oil and vinegar, turning it over every two hours, or something of the kind. After that you had to simmer it gently. Therefore, when I was confronted with four decapitated and sinewy old hens, I had a flash of inspiration.

Johnny and I had, from time to time, been invited by our friends to the most sumptuous meals in their homes. Some were lucky enough to have an Italian chef, others had nothing but their own fairy fingers, guided by a talent for turning out the most divine concoctions. Second only to the gastronomic marvels they produced was their gift for appearing unruffled from the kitchen to greet their guests, calmly dispensing drinks while the dinner apparently looked after itself. This had such a demoralising effect on me that I felt quite incapable of issuing a return invitation. I could never aspire to such perfection and I buried my head in the sand of my defection, letting the weeks turn into months without attempting to return my friends' hospitality.

Now I could convert my four hoary old birds into spring chicken that would melt in the mouth. I would work off all my overdue invitations at one fell swoop and offer them a delicious feast. Quickly I telephoned everybody and they could all come; the party was fixed for the following evening. We were to be 12 to dinner.

I arranged with my invaluable Mrs Ridd, who came from the village once a week and scrubbed and polished the whole house in a day, that she would come up in the evening to help me dish up and to wash up. Then I planned my menu. We would start with grapefruit, which I happened to have. This would be followed by the *pièce de résistance*, my succulent birds, and rounded off by a vast fruit salad and two of Hilary's heavenly lemon meringue pies, which she makes better than anyone else I know. With the birds, we would have Brussels sprouts, fresh from the garden, and puréed potatoes.

The whole household helped with the plucking and drawing and I plunged my fowls into an enormous fish kettle filled with oil and vinegar, turning them from time to time with religious fervour. There I left them overnight.

The next day was one of intense activity and Johnny's farm work received scant attention. I was determined to do the thing in style and the house was thrown into a turmoil. The back kitchen had to be hastily transformed into a dining-room, pictures and curtains hung, candles found, wines purchased, flowers produced from nowhere, and Johnny had to get in a supply of logs for the huge fireplace.

Filled with visions of past grandeur, I decided to use the old de Pfeffel family silver, which I had inherited from my mother. It seemed a pity that it should never see the light of day – now was the perfect occasion. It hadn't been unearthed for so long that when I dug it out not only did every knife and fork and spoon have to be polished, but the knife blades, which had been fashioned long before stainless steel was thought of, flaunted patches of rust which had to be removed. Nothing that we tried had any effect; finally Mumpti was taken off the job of putting a new concrete floor in the barn and spent the entire afternoon cleaning the blades on Johnny's grindstone.

It took him hours, but he did the trick. Meanwhile my best

dinner service was carried through the house to the kitchen from the dairy where it was stored, wreathed in dust, and given a good wash.

The afternoon passed swiftly into early evening; my fowls were simmering away on the stove, and I was peeling a mountain of potatoes while Hilary coped with the lemon meringue. Johnny kept on appearing maddeningly in the kitchen every few minutes to remind me of the zero hour, when our guests were due.

Everything seemed to be going according to plan, until I removed the lid of the cast iron cauldron in order to prick the birds with a fork to see if they were tender – and discovered that there were no birds to prick. They had completely disintegrated; there was nothing but bits of wing and breast and leg floating about in gallons of stock. My immediate reaction at all times of crisis is to find Johnny. He was lighting the fire in the back kitchen. The only thing to do, he told me, was to tip everything through a strainer and turn it into curried chicken.

I had never made curried chicken, so I dived into Mrs Beeton and found a recipe. I put on rice to boil and set about the finicky job of separating the rapidly cooling bits of meat from the conglomeration of bones. I was all thumbs and perspiration, there was an hour to go and I was rapidly losing my head. Thank goodness Mrs Ridd had arrived and Hilary was laying the table. I asked Mrs Ridd to deal with the sprouts and open the tins of fruit salad.

'Where are the sprouts?' she inquired.

They were, of course, still in the garden, as yet unpicked. Just then Johnny popped his head round the door to remind me of the time and I could have thrown the whole dinner at him, but instead I said, 'Bring me the sack of turnips which the deer have nibbled.'

'We will have mashed turnip,' I told Mrs Ridd.

The rice was ready and I strained it into a colander and turned the cold tap on to it, as instructed, to separate the grains. While I was doing this I remembered the grapefruit, so I dumped the colander on the draining board and dived into the larder for them. My mother had taught me how to prepare grapefruit.

'It is worth taking a little extra trouble,' she had said. 'Never serve grapefruit without removing all the skins from between each section. First you must cut round the rim with a curved knife, then you remove the core and then you carefully slide your knife down on either side of the skins and lift them out. It is slovenly to bring grapefruit to the table with the skins still in and just loosening them is not sufficient. Such a habit would never be tolerated in France.'

With training like this, it never entered my mind to do anything else. With 40 minutes to go, I cut the six grapefruit in half and started battling with the skins. I got through nine halves before Johnny ordered me up to change; the remaining three were still untouched, complete with cores and not even loosened from the peel. I fled through the house into the back kitchen with my 12 halves on a tray and carefully deposited the uncut ones in Johnny's, Hilary's and my own places at table. Then I bolted back to the kitchen before Johnny caught sight of me, and gave desperate instructions to Mrs Ridd.

'Will you please mash the boiled potatoes and make the curry sauce? The stock for the sauce is in that big cauldron and you take a pint and mix in the curry powder – the recipe's in the book – and then you put the pieces of chicken into the sauce. I'll be back in a moment.'

It was many moments before I was back, because I was still hunting for a pair of unladdered stockings when the guests arrived. Johnny held the fort, as he invariably does, while I pounded between bathroom and bedroom. Then I came down and was absorbed into the vortex of conversation and drinks. Finally I excused myself and padded along to the kitchen in a happy-go-lucky frame of mind.

'Have you made the sauce?' I asked cheerfully.

'Yes,' said Mrs Ridd, 'and put in the chicken. It's in that big saucepan keeping warm, but it looks rather peculiar.'

I peered in. Mrs Ridd hadn't brought her glasses, so she couldn't read the recipe and had tried to remember what I had gabbled at her. Her recollection was that she must mix the curry powder with the stock in the cauldron and she had mixed it with the entire quantity – about a gallon of it – and then popped in the chicken. What I beheld was soup with a few fragments of meat floating in it.

We strained the chicken pulp, which had not the slightest taste of curry and might well have been straw, and placed it in the centre of a large dish. Then I looked in the bottom of the oven for the rice to arrange tastefully around the mess in the middle, only to discover it was still reposing on the draining board, stone cold. Mrs Ridd assured me she had mashed the potatoes. Indeed she had. She had done just as I said. I had omitted to mention the addition of butter and milk and she had churned them up with the masher – they were potatoes, mashed. The deer-bitten turnips were similarly mashed, and rather stringy.

We served the gallon of curry sauce as soup; it became 'court-bouillon à la Nethercote' and was quite revolting. But we started off, of course, with the grapefruit. Our eight guests and Mumpti made short work of their dissected portions and laid down their spoons while Johnny, Hilary and I were still digging away at the first or second section as if we were trying to prise a limpet from a rock. It wasn't long before we gave up and left them uneaten.

The dismal meal proceeded and I didn't dare look at Johnny, who told me later that he had never eaten such a shocking dinner in his life. The only saving grace was Hilary's lemon meringue pie, which was delicious and at last enabled the poor guests to find words of praise for what was set before them. But I must record that one hero (a bachelor who lived on his own) took a second helping of the straw and cold rice and thereby earned my undying gratitude.

That was my last dinner party. However, the night ended better than it had begun, for Johnny kept the glasses well filled and the party became very merry and went on until 4.00am. Around midnight he fried eggs and bacon over the blazing fire in the middle-kitchen, balancing my mother's copper frying pans precariously on the logs and nearly roasting himself in the process. All in all, I believe our guests didn't carry away too bad an impression of their evening.

This whole sorry tale shows me up as a complete nitwit. But the 'dining-room' did look lovely, with the beautiful old silver gleaming in the light from the candles and the log fire. No-one could have imagined how it had looked that very morning. There was one other redeeming feature; the wines, chosen by Johnny, were good. 'Mine Host' at the Royal Oak in Winsford is a connoisseur and keeps an excellent cellar, hardly to be bettered in a big city.

We have never known what to do with our old hens, since we cannot bring ourselves to kill them.

Johnny will say to me, 'I can't think why you go on buying expensive meat from the butcher when we could be eating our old boilers. Do you realise, my dear girl, what I am paying in corn bills to keep them? Does it ever occur to you that it costs us about £3 an egg?'

'Right,' I reply. 'If you will wring their necks, I'll pluck them and draw them and cook them. You can bring me two a week.'

There is a pause. 'Well, perhaps,' he murmurs, 'it would be as well to wait until the children are home and we can finish them all off during the holidays.'

'That's a good idea,' I agree, and the holidays come and go and no further mention is made of the dear old sweeties.

There finally came a day when we both realised that something would have to be done about the old faithfuls we had brought with us from Surrey. Miraculously, the perfect solution presented itself. Johnny met a poultry dealer called Mr Baker, who was prepared to collect them alive and take them away. It was Saturday and he arranged to come for them on the following Tuesday. He would back his van up to the door of the deep litter house and all we would have to do would be to catch them and transfer them to the van.

The hens hadn't laid an egg for weeks, or certainly not more than half a dozen between the 25 of them in the last month. They looked a sorry sight, for they were moulting. Their feathers were bedraggled, their eyes dull, their combs a pallid purplish pink. We were afraid Mr Baker would offer us nothing at all for them and we might have to pay him for taking them away, but no matter, we would be rid of them without having to kill them.

When I fed them that afternoon I felt terrible as they ran up to me so trustingly. I recognised one after the other and thought,

150

'There's old Henrietta who hatched out her chicks on the shelf in the bicycle shed, and that's poor Old Crone who sat for five weeks on addled ducks' eggs in the woodpile before we found her. And here's my sweet little Broken Wing, who never grew as big as the others but always kept up with them so gamely, and darling Jessica who defended her gosling from the fox, and old Three Claws who lost one in a gin trap in Staddon Wood.'

Here they all were, not knowing what awaited them, and I felt like a traitor.

I had no need to worry, for they knew how to take care of themselves. They must have held an emergency meeting in the deep litter house that night.

Early on the Sunday morning we were awakened by the surprising sound of cackling.

'Oh dear!' I thought guiltily, 'One of them has laid.'

The cackles went on almost without a break, until we decided that something must be wrong and perhaps a hen had got caught up in some wire netting. We dressed hastily and went off to investigate.

An amazing sight met our eyes. The nesting boxes were full of laying birds, piled one on top of the other, with a queue waiting to take their places. Those who had already been successful were all cackling their heads off while their sisters pushed and strained with the utmost concentration. Lovely brown eggs nestled in every box. Moreover, the hens themselves had undergone a complete transformation. Their feathers were sleek and gleaming, their combs scarlet, their eyes bright.

When we had recovered our breath we rushed to the phone and cancelled Mr Baker.

The hens went on laying madly until they were quite confident of their reprieve, after which they settled contentedly back into their old life of idleness and comfort, just laying an occasional egg for form's sake. In the end Mr Baker did fetch them, about three months later, sneaking up on them unawares with his van. But Prissy, one of my dear old brown sweeties, managed to fly out of the small space between the top of the hen-house door and roof of the van and escape. She was at least 11 years old when she died.

Whether laying or not, and no matter how bad the weather was, the poultry still had to be fed and tended. I would sally forth across the yard with my hen buckets, attired like an old scarecrow. In fact I still do so and am sometimes reminded of a conversation I once had with a young girl called Betty, who at one time cycled up from the village to help with the housework. Her previous employer had been Lady Savery.

'I liked it there,' she told me. 'It was proper – if only I hadn't had to say, "Yes, Lady Savery," "No, Sir Reginald," from morning to night. It's all very well to call them by their titles first thing in the morning, but not all day long.'

Betty informed me with relish that her Ladyship, when she fed her hens, used to wear Sir Reginald's gumboots, three sizes too big for her, and a disreputable old raincoat which was too small and wouldn't meet in front, so she wore an apron on top to close the gap.

'That's just like me!' I laughed, 'I always wear my husband's gumboots and his cap and a dirty old raincoat tied round my middle with string.'

There was a pregnant pause and then she volunteered, 'Well yes … er … but then, you see, it's all right for you, but *she's* a lady!'

CHAPTER 22

Ilona, Maria and Miss Collins

Some time after the Hungarian revolution of 1956 I wrote to a refugee camp in the Midlands, offering employment at Nethercote. After a while the secretary phoned me one evening to propose a couple called Istvan and Ilona Tomacs. She said the man had told the interpreter that he was fully conversant with all farm work and the woman said she was a capable housewife. Johnny and I agreed to have them on a month's trial on either side.

They arrived from Birmingham and I picked them up at Minehead station. Istvan spoke no word of any language except Hungarian and Ilona, apart from Hungarian, knew a few words of Russian, which she had learnt after the war from the soldiers quartered in her village.

I hadn't spoken Russian for nearly 30 years, but it did afford us a sketchy means of contact. Very often, unfortunately, our respective vocabularies didn't coincide and Ilona and I became adept at dumb crambo. It was very difficult for us to understand one another at first and it was about a fortnight before we were able to carry on a more or less coherent conversation, half in Russian and half in Hungarian, with the aid of a very inadequate 'Vocabulary' provided by the refugee organisation. Hungarian dictionaries were unobtainable.

As for Johnny, the situation was hopeless. He had no means of communicating with Istvan except by signs, although the latter would hopefully launch himself into a long discourse in Hungarian. Often, in order to sort out some tangle, both Ilona and I would have to be summoned from the house. Istvan would then go into a long-winded explanation to Ilona, who would turn it into halting Russian for me, punctuated with the gesticulations of a Punch and Judy show, and I would then translate for Johnny. It was time-wasting and nerve-racking.

It was a while before I understood Ilona sufficiently to grasp that she and Istvan were not the married couple I had supposed them to be. Although their names were indeed both Tomacs, they were brother and sister-in-law. She was married to Istvan's elder brother, who had remained in Hungary. However they appeared to have no objection to the double bed into which I had thrust them on arrival and continued cosily to share it.

It didn't take Johnny more than a few minutes to find out that Istvan knew little or nothing about farming, was unable to drive a tractor and was idle besides. If unsupervised, he would sit on the river bank dabbling his feet in the water and chewing a bit of grass instead of getting on with whatever job he was meant to be doing.

Ilona, on the other hand, was all that she claimed to be and I found her a tower of strength – literally, for she was a sturdy country girl, tough and muscular, and was used to working in the fields. It was a wonder to see her at haymaking, running with enormous loads held high on her pitchfork and pitching them effortlessly onto the top of the trailer. She could easily keep up with the men and used to chide Arthur and call to him in Hungarian to get a move on. He would pull her leg in English and they were great pals, in spite of the language barrier.

Once I was able to understand her, she explained to me that her widowed mother had owned a small farm, but the communist government had commandeered it. They were thus deprived of their means of support and were desperate. It so happened that her mother knew a man who was friendly with an important personage in the government, so she pleaded with him to use his influence to have her farm returned to her. He agreed to try on the condition that if he succeeded she would give him Ilona as his wife. Thus it came about that at the age of 18 she married what she described to me as 'an old man of 48'. During the uprising she gave him the slip and escaped across the frontier with his younger and more attractive brother.

She was just as efficient in the house as she was out of doors and Johnny and I started thinking how wonderful it would be if only we could get rid of Istvan and keep Ilona. Then one day, after they had been with us less than three weeks, I found her in floods of tears. She explained between gulps that Istvan didn't like country life and wished to go back to Birmingham, where he could work in a factory.

I tried to console her, although I couldn't understand the reason for her tears, and told her how sorry we would be to lose them both. At this she protested vehemently and her sobs redoubled. She told me in Russian that she hated the sight of him and never wanted to see him again and would I please keep her with me and let him go alone?

This seemed too good to be true. We agreed with alacrity to her proposal and Istvan departed. We turned the back kitchen into a bedsitter for her and lent her a wireless on which she could listen to the BBC Hungarian broadcasts. At first she was happy and all went well, but apart from these short broadcasts, and the musical items, the wireless was useless to her. Nor could she read any books or newspapers and we had no television, so she had nothing to do in her free time. Naturally she felt lonely, cut off from her own people.

She was genuinely devoted to me and looked on me as a combination of mother, sister and friend. She was demonstrative in her gratitude for the least thing I did for her and would often fling her arms round me and hug me. Singing and laughing one moment, she would be moody and silent the next and these periods of depression increased.

One day she asked me if I would phone the Hungarian priest at the refugee camp so that she could speak to him. She called him the *Popa*. I put the call through to the Midlands that evening, but was told by the camp secretary that the priest was only available during the day. So the following day I got through to him and she prattled away in excited Hungarian. Her call lasted 20 minutes, with the pips sounding like hammer blows in my ears as the cost mounted, but she seemed more cheerful as a result.

A few days later, however, she again asked to speak to the *Popa* and burst into tears when I appeared to hesitate. Once more I phoned the camp and she embarked on a lively and interminable harangue. The *Popa* got in a few words from time to time, only to be interrupted as she launched herself into another almost hysterical outburst.

She refused to tell me what the trouble was and was soon asking to call the *Popa* every two or three days. So I got on to the camp secretary and asked her if she could enlighten me.

She told me she thought Ilona had some spiritual problem and would never be happy until it was resolved. She was an ardent Catholic and I gathered she had religious scruples about her irregular association with Istvan, but she was lonely without him and missed him more and more.

Finally, after another phone call, she announced that the *Popa* was arriving at Nethercote the following morning. He would do the return journey in one day, she said. Of course she had no idea of the distance and it was obvious he would have to spend the night with us. I prepared a room for him, found the most likely train in the timetable and met him at Dulverton.

Apart from Hungarian, he spoke a little German, so we managed the conversation quite successfully, larding it with Latin when German failed us. My German was better than his, but of course he could run rings round me in Latin, though I proudly dug up *cibus* and *gallinai* when we went together to feed the hens.

At last my long-buried education was coming in handy and could provide an answer to the occasional exasperated question, 'What is the use of an Oxford degree if you can't tell a chisel from a screwdriver?' Ilona would talk vigorously to the *Popa* at great length in Hungarian, he would then put the gist of her harangue to me in German, I would pass it on to Johnny in English and then respond to Ilona in Russian. Babel had nothing on Nethercote. By then the original subject of the conversation had become so distorted by misunderstandings and faulty translation that we had lost sight of our objective.

From the moment the *Popa* entered the house Ilona removed her shoes and went about barefoot until he left.

'You can't wear shoes in the presence of God,' she told me.

It was only later that I discovered that you can't eat in the presence of God either, and by then poor Ilona must have been half-starved.

I had thought it a good idea to let the priest have his meals with her in the back kitchen, where they could discuss her spiritual problems in peace. So I had loaded trays with food for them both, which she had carried in. I didn't go to her room until the next day, after he had departed; it was then that I found all her own food untouched. Later she informed me that her duty was to serve him, but not to eat in his company. I couldn't make out why she hadn't eaten at night, after he had retired; perhaps the food was too unappetising by then, or the emotional upheaval too great.

She was certainly in no fit state to enter into any explanations when I returned from driving the *Popa* to Dulverton. Tommie greeted me with the news that as soon as we had been lost to view she had gone into violent hysterics, beating her breast, tearing her hair and wailing so that her shrieks echoed through the house. She had done her best to quieten her, but had failed and had finally left her to it in her room. For almost an hour she had been forced to listen to the banshee wailing, and then suddenly all was quiet. On investigating, she had found Ilona collapsed on the bed, having fallen into an exhausted sleep.

She was still in that position when I got back. It was then that my eye fell on all the uneaten food. We quickly prepared an attractive meal for her and left it by her bedside and in due course she reappeared and went on with her work, quite merry and bright, having done full justice to her lunch.

On the way to the station the *Popa* had told me that he thought Ilona was suffering from a psychological disturbance, which was the natural result of the terrible experiences she had gone through during the ill-fated revolt, coupled with a feeling of loneliness and uprootal and a longing for news from home. This was only too understandable, but there was little I could do to help until she knew English well enough to share more fully in the life of the community. He suggested that meanwhile, if it were possible for us to obtain from the camp another Hungarian woman to keep her company, things might rapidly improve.

We didn't need any extra help for Tommie was still with us at that time, but she was thinking of going back to nursing and I didn't want to lose Ilona. So Johnny and I talked it over and decided to take the priest's advice and allow her to return to the camp and find herself a companion.

Although there were thousands of unfortunate Hungarians in need of work and good homes, it was difficult to find anyone willing to settle in the country. Many of the refugees belonged to the professional classes, others had young families or husbands working in factories, and the great majority were understandably reluctant to live away from their own countrymen, particularly if they had to exchange the bustle of city life for the rigours of the wilds. There were very few unattached women with a country background.

Ilona was away three days and returned with Maria. I had a shock when I saw her. She had a vacant stare, lank greasy locks trailing down her back, tufts of hair sprouting from warts all over her face and neck, and against all the odds of probability, in view of her unprepossessing appearance, she looked suspiciously rotund in front.

Ilona pushed her forward, to the accompaniment of a

running commentary in Russian and broken English, quelling my protests with the assurance that Maria couldn't understand a word she said.

'She not beautiful. She best I find, other womans no good, all have man not leave. Maria not beautiful, not clever, but she want come.'

I soon realised that she was right when she said Maria couldn't understand, for she couldn't even understand her own language and bungled everything Ilona asked her to do. I found the only thing she could manage was dusting, which she really enjoyed, so I let her spend all day going round the house with a duster.

She was so mentally slow it was impossible to teach her anything. In spite of the months she had spent in England and the time she lived with us, she never learnt a word of English, and unless Ilona was there I had to struggle with the Hungarian vocabulary. She was unspeakably dirty and never went near the bathroom. After two months I had to order her to wash her hair and stand over her while she did so.

We would have given anything to get rid of her, but where was she to go? I couldn't possible recommend her to anyone else. I felt sorry for her and hadn't the strength of mind to send her back to the refugee camp, where so many of her fellow Hungarians were still hopelessly waiting for resettlement.

To cap everything, I had to go to Paris with my sister Den to clean up the house of our old aunt Yvonne de Pfeffel, whose memory was failing and whom we had brought over to England. While I was in France, Johnny wrote to say that Ilona had joined Istvan in Birmingham, bequeathing us Maria as a legacy. He enclosed a note to me from Ilona saying she loved me but couldn't live without him.

In the end we got rid of Maria in the most unexpected way. A strange male Hungarian arrived at Nethercote out of the blue, asking for her. He said she was his 'lady friend' and closeted himself with her in the back kitchen. Afternoon turned into evening and he showed no sign of leaving. Eventually I informed him that the house was full, which was quite true. I told him we would be unable to put him up for the night; he must either walk into the village to find accommodation or try Mrs Stevens (who took in paying guests), if she had room. Alternatively, he could sleep in the manger in the stable.

He answered airily, 'OK, me not need, me sleep with lady friend, she like wife to me!'

I explained that this was not the custom in England, that all my children were at home and I couldn't allow such an arrangement, and bundled him into the stable. But I have no doubt that as soon as we were all in bed he took advantage of the outside door into the back kitchen.

His visit proved fruitful nonetheless, for a few days after his departure Maria announced that he had a job in Bristol and she was off to join him.

After Tommie left I was without help except for Mrs Ridd once a week, and there were often times when she was unable to come for several weeks.

I tried advertising and replying to advertisements and spent many wasted hours writing out lyrical descriptions of the glories of Nethercote, but it was hopeless – our remoteness was a fatal drawback. But I had noticed an advertisement which kept appearing with monotonous regularity. It requested a home for a lady and her three well-behaved cats, in exchange for housework and a small remuneration.

I had answered so many advertisements without even a reply, despite the stamped envelopes I enclosed, that I decided I might as well have a stab at this one, since prospective employers would hardly be tumbling over each other to acquire the cats. Johnny issued dire warnings of the consequences, but I was physically and mentally exhausted with housework and was prepared to put up with an entire menagerie if need be.

The deal was concluded and a few weeks later the advertiser, Miss Collins, arrived at Dulverton station with innumerable cases and crates and rather the worse for wear, since she had travelled for many hours in the railway van with her cats, who would feel frightened if she deserted them. There were two toms, Billy and Bunter, and a female, Flossie. She told us she had had them since they were kittens and they were all she had in the world. They were house-trained, she added, and she was used to having them always with her, though she quite understood it would be difficult in someone else's home and was willing to keep them shut in and take them for walks in her free time.

Needless to say, they resisted all her attempts to confine them; we could never be sure where they were. They followed her into the kitchen, sending all our dogs into a frenzy, and woke us at night with blood-curdling yowls. I spent my time hiding in corners out of Johnny's sight.

Miss Collins believed in what she called natural selection among animals and made no attempt to segregate Flossie when she was in season. The two tom cats engaged one another in mortal combat and she was for ever borrowing cotton wool and Dettol to dress their wounds.

She would report for work in the morning and announce,

'Bunter has nearly scratched out Billy's eye again!'

Johnny washed his hands of the whole affair and declared that he would divorce me or find himself another job if I didn't get rid of her before Flossie's kittens arrived. It was an ultimatum which put me in a quandary, since she had nowhere to go. In addition to the cats, she was handicapped by a squint and by a lisp which made it impossible for me, with my deafness, to understand a word she said. She was obliged to write me notes. Her very disabilities aroused my compassion and sapped my resolution. She was also quite hopeless at housework and cooking.

She admitted this cheerfully, adding, 'My parents ought to have given me some training, oughtn't they? They never trained me for anything. How did they think I would be able to earn our living after they were gone? It was very thoughtless of them.'

I advised her to part with the cats, since they were the chief stumbling block in her attempts to get a job, but her eyes filled with tears and she said her life would be quite empty without them and she would sooner starve. That was all very well, but I couldn't stand by and watch it happen.

Time was running out on me, as Flossie's ample curves developed, when I was saved by the bell. Miss Collins informed me that the cats weren't happy at Nethercote and she had decided to use her savings in renting a caravan for herself and her dear pussies, somewhere near a big town where she could work in hotels (which? I wondered), and make a nice home for Billy, Bunter, Flossie and the little Billets or Buntlets.

I recommended a busy seaside resort absolutely teeming with hotels, at least a hundred miles away, and she went off to make arrangements, leaving me to look after the cats. They departed in the nick of time, for she wrote to tell me that Flossie had had four darling little kittens the evening after they took over the caravan.

CHAPTER 23

Tante Yvonne

Our French Tante Yvonne, my mother's only sister, was within a few weeks of her 74th birthday when my sisters and I brought her to England from Paris. She was a doctor and had never married; she had devoted most of her adult life until her retirement to the Children's Hospital, where she was *Chef de Laboratoire*, and had given her services free for years. She was now losing her memory and we felt it was no longer possible for her to live alone. She spoke English fluently, but with a strong French accent.

Physically, she was extraordinarily tough; she had been a good mountaineer in her youth and had been accustomed all her life to walking many miles a day. She hardly ever travelled in Paris by metro or bus, preferring to use her legs, and would walk from one end of the capital to the other and miles out into the suburbs and back at weekends, right up to the time when she came to live in England.

She started by staying with each of the four sisters in turn, and at the beginning of June 1957 Den brought her to Nethercote from London.

She loved the country and the dogs and was eager to set off on long tramps, but her memory played tricks on her. She didn't always realise where she was and sometimes fancied that she was staying with friends in the countryside in France. This delusion was helped by the fact that we spoke to her in French. Another difficulty was that she imagined she recognised particular landmarks and knew where she was, whereas this was, in fact, her first visit to Somerset. The moor was practically at our doorstep, stretching out of sight for miles, and we soon realised, though not fully, the danger of letting her wander off alone.

Den went back to London almost at once, and on 4 June, not only did our Hungarian refugees arrive, but our sheepdog bitch, Lassie, had eight puppies, so on the following day chaos reigned and I was too busy coping with the monkey house to keep Tante Yvonne constantly with me. It was to prove a fateful day, as I recorded in a letter to the children that evening.

As I write, we are in the middle of the most terrific drama and I only hope it turns out all right. I have been nearly out of my mind all day with worry, but I feel a little more hopeful now that the police have the matter in hand.

What has happened is that I took Tante Yvonne to the bottom of the path leading up onto Bye Common at 11.30 this morning and sent her off for a little walk, accompanied by two of the terriers, Crumpy and Nina. I told her to go to the top of the path, admire the view, and then come down again the same way, never losing sight of the farm so she couldn't go wrong. This was nine and a half hours ago and she hasn't come back – neither have Crumpy and Nina.

At first we thought she was having a little walk round

and didn't worry. But at lunchtime we all started to hunt in every direction leading away from the top of Bye – and she could have gone in any direction. I was nearly frantic with anxiety. Daddy was ploughing far away on the Brakes and had taken sandwiches with him. So I took the Ford and drove down to Larcombe Foot and through Winsford and up Ash Lane, in case she had made her way right across Bye Common and come out there through Great Ash fields. This is precisely what she did do, I must have missed her by a few minutes. When I got home Tommie set out over Bye on foot, crossed into Ash Lane, went on to Comer's Cross, and came back over Room Hill, arriving home exhausted. Meanwhile Major and Mrs Eyre were keeping a constant watch on Bye from their house at Larcombe Foot, scanning the hillside through binoculars.

By the time Tommie returned, I had phoned PC Short at Winsford and reinforcements were on their way. Without stopping to draw breath, Tommie, tired as she was, set off to fetch Daddy from the Brakes. It was well after 4.00pm by then and soon things really began to get cracking. Police came from Winsford, Exford and Dulverton, in cars and on motorcycles. The Devon and Somerset Constabulary converged on Nethercote in carloads from Minehead, Taunton and from as far as Bridgwater and with them came a tracker dog, an Alsatian, with his handler, who had come all the way from Glastonbury.

I found the handler a cardigan which Tante Yvonne had worn this morning and he gave it to the dog to sniff. Then we watched him set off on the track up onto Bye

Common with his nose to the ground, followed by his handler, and behind them came policemen, slowly puffing up the steep path. It was the most thrilling sight. He would stop from time to time to nose around, and then proceed quickly on his way, waiting every now and then for his handler to catch up with him. I knew the aunt had gone that way, for I had watched her. The dog didn't know, but there he was, picking up her track step by step.

Before he had reached the top of the path, where it vanished over the horizon, word came through by phone that she had been seen at Comer's Cross several hours earlier. Daddy jumped on Stan's motorcycle and went speeding up the track to Bye to tell the police. They came down again and took the dog by car to Comer's Cross to pick up the scent there, where it would be fresher. Shortly afterwards, they got a message to say Farmer Hawkins had spoken to her in Withypool at 3.10pm. She had been walking at a brisk pace with the dogs and had remarked to him what a lovely day it was. The police with the dog drove on to Withypool, where they were told she had last been seen heading towards Sandyway. They took the dog past the cattle grid the other side of the village and he picked up the scent and was off on the trail. Daddy was there in the Ford.

It was then about 8.00pm and the news was spreading like wildfire through the villages. Two hours have gone by since I began this letter, for I have been answering the phone continually. People have been ringing me up to ask if they could help by going out to search; but I said no, because I thought the police would prefer to do things their own way and the more people there were about, the more difficult it would be for the dog to follow the scent.

The police have set up their headquarters at the Royal Oak at Withypool and have been ringing me up every half hour to ask if I have any news and to tell me the latest information they have. They keep on telling me not to worry and that they will find her, and I must say I feel more cheerful now they are in charge; they are so very calm and efficient and encouraging. It is dark now and I hope they find her soon.

Continued next day

I will continue from where I left off last night. By 10pm Tante Yvonne still hadn't been found. By then, speed-cop police cars with walkie-talkies had arrived from Bridgwater and were covering the roads in all directions from Withypool. I was nearly demented, not only about the poor old aunt, who had eaten nothing since a plate of cornflakes at breakfast, but also about Crumpy and Nina, who are unused to traffic and were out on the roads in the dark and might get run over.

Daddy came home at 1.00am, gulped down some food and saddled Sunshine. Then he went off to search the fields and moor around Landacre, thinking the dogs might hear the horse and that if he kept on calling them and whistling they would come. He took a rug with him in case he found her, because it had been raining and had turned quite chilly. He searched all night and so did the police and also many other people, like Bob Barrow, the AA man, who walked all night with the handler and his dog. When at daybreak there was still no sign of her, all the special constables were called out; men like Fred Hayes, farmers and others who are reserve members of the police force and are called upon in emergencies. They ranged the countryside and the moor on horseback. Fred Hayes was called out at 5.00am.

At 8.00am, Daddy came back on Sunshine. He said people were standing outside their houses at 2.30 in Withypool when he rode through, and were still outside their houses at 5.00 this morning! Somewhere around 8.00am Inspector Butt, of Minehead, who was in charge of operations, decided to call out the Army to search the moor. He was on the phone to the Western Region Depots when he received the news which made it unnecessary.

Daddy was having breakfast before setting off again and Fred Hayes, who had ridden down over Room Hill, was breakfasting with us, when the police phoned. They said a postman had seen two white dogs in the bracken the other side of the river and a long way from the road, at a place called Pickedstones, and he thought he could make out the shape of someone lying in the bracken. The two police cars were making at once for the place. It is some miles beyond Landacre and about seven miles from here as the crow flies, and must have been at least 15 by the route she had taken.

They told us later that they had to leave the cars on the road, cross the river and make their way through the bracken, where, sure enough, they found the aunt, with Crumpy and Nina on guard. Crumpy had constituted herself her bodyguard, defender and protector. Small as she is, as soon as the police approached she flew at the nearest one, a speed-cop from Bridgwater, and bit him! The aunt was lying there, completely exhausted, soaked to the skin and covered with mud. She had either sprained or broken an ankle and the police had to carry her along the river bank and across a bridge. They think she must have tried to cross the river, slipped and hurt her ankle and then dragged herself the rest of the way across and through the bracken on the other side. She lay there all night with the dogs, while it rained and the temperature dropped. Fortunately she had a coat over her thin dress.

By 10.30am she was back at Nethercote, after 23 hours on the spree! She remembers hardly anything at all but has a hazy recollection of hugging the dogs in turn – to keep them warm, she explained! She had no idea she had been gone since yesterday and still hasn't grasped it. She was in a bad way when the police brought her home. Tommie peeled off her muddy clothes and put her to bed with a hot bottle. At lunchtime I crept into her room and found her sitting up in bed, rosy cheeked and smiling. She asked me the time, and when she heard it was one o'clock she cried, "Good heavens, what am I doing in bed at this hour? I must get up at once!" and so saying, she scrambled out of bed and I was only just in time to stop her from putting her injured foot to the floor. She is the most incredibly tough and resilient old lady.

She has been dozing most of the day, with Crumpy lying on her bed and growling at anyone who comes into the room, including Daddy and Tommie. The police told us that if the dogs had not (a) kept her warm through

171

the night, or at least prevented her from dying from exposure in her soaking clothes, and (b) stayed near her so the postman was able to spot their white bodies in the bracken, she could have lain there until she died and they might never have found her, or not found her until it was too late. Another 24 hours and she would probably have been dead.

In a way Tante Yvonne saved her own life because of her love for dogs. If she hadn't made such friends of them after only three days at Nethercote, they would never have followed her on her walk; and even if they had, they might not have remained with her all night in the rain and cold, when they could so easily have found their way home.

The police were unremitting in their efforts and no praise could do justice to them, or to all the other helpers who came to the rescue. Even Miss Vesey at the telephone exchange in Winsford played a part in the drama, chipping in with the latest news as her busy fingers linked our calls.

The ankle turned out to be only sprained and Tante Yvonne made a speedy recovery. She was soon anxious to undertake another '*petite promenade*' and we could never let her out of our sight for a moment.

CHAPTER 24

Lassie was a flirt

Lassie was the most outrageous flirt. She was a lovely looking collie bitch, red with white markings, and never lacked admirers. Chief among them was Tom's sheepdog, Kylie. He was a magnificent dog, also red and white, so they always had beautiful puppies, with burnished glossy coats. Kylie could clear any wall which parted him from his beloved, and as Lassie seemed able to spirit herself through a three inch gap of window we were continually being presented with unplanned litters.

Lassie's first husband had, unknown to us, paid her his homage before we bought her, and to our astonishment she produced a litter of whippets. Inquiries of her breeder elicited the fact that he had once caught a whippet descending the vertical ladder leading to the loft in which she was confined. Nature will outwit all our precautions – ably abetted by Tom. He has a genius for accidentally leaving loopholes; out of sympathy for Kylie, I suspect.

Fortunately for us, Lassie's progeny were good workers and their owners were satisfied and recommended us to their friends. Even so, the supply tended to exceed the demand and reluctantly we were compelled to knock some of the little bitch puppies on the head at birth. Poor Arthur was always landed with this horrible job, which we couldn't possibly face, but one or other of us had to pick out the victims and it was a task we all dreaded. It is best done as soon as possible after the puppies are born.

We put down the bitches rather than the dogs because the former are more difficult to sell. Twice a year a bitch has to be segregated for three weeks, unless you want a litter. Invariably this period occurs just when she is most urgently needed for working the sheep. If her master decides to use her, he lives to regret it, for a dog seems to materialise out of the ground and off they go together. Therefore farmers tend to choose a dog, since they can rely on his help the whole year round. By the time Lassie died of old age at 13 half the farms on Exmoor and some of the homes in Winsford and, indeed, as far afield as Cornwall were graced by red and white sheepdogs.

Although Kylie was Lassie's 'steady' she has had a few unsteadies, among whom was Davie, a yellow and white collie who sired one of her litters. Davie comes from a farm three miles away. He is growing old and hasn't paid us a visit for some time now, but in his heyday he would materialise unobtrusively before we knew ourselves that one of our bitches was coming into season.

I say unobtrusively because he just lay all day concealed in the shelter of some bushes or a hedge, probably because Leader gave him short shrift if he scented or glimpsed him. By looking carefully, we could just make out his ears, or his white plumed tail flickering among the leaves, as he kept up his patient vigil, hour after hour and day after day.

Minky, our black Labrador, was the object of his adoration, and he took no notice of the other bitches until after her death. Leader used to sleep in the kitchen at night and Shep in Arthur's room, which left the field clear for Davie. He would then venture forth from his hiding place and take up his position outside the boudoir of his beloved.

We once shut Minky up inside a shooting brake in our yard; it was securely closed but there was a small pane of glass missing from the very top of the back door, with no purchase at all for climbing purposes. I looked out of a window early the next morning and spied Davie in the act of squirming through and was just in time to haul him out by his hind legs. Poor Davie. He never managed to father any of Minky's puppies, although he paid her court for several years.

He became a real problem because he was so lovelorn he took up permanent quarters at Nethercote at the appropriate times and didn't bother to go home for food. I knew I must on no account feed him if there was to be any hope of his forsaking us and I would harden my heart and let several days go by. It had no effect. Davie, after several cold and hungry days and nights of rain or frost spent out in the open, would still be there, watching me feed the other dogs from his vantage point with pleading eyes. It was more than I could bear and I always ended by taking him something.

After Leader died he grew bolder. He would leave his hide and come up to me expectantly, his tail wagging. How could I possibly starve him? Johnny took him home by car countless times, but he was back over hill and combe before Johnny could get home by road.

His master told us that we must chase him away with a stick, but neither of us could do it, although we each urged the other to be firm. We foresaw the moment when we would have him for ever. Fortunately Tommie and Arthur had more strength of mind and drove him away. Johnny and

175

I would keep well out of sight in order not to be associated with such treachery.

We have had so many litters of puppies, some purposely but most of them through a slap-happy lack of precaution, that I have lost count.

With every new litter it is the same. Johnny gazes at the small fluffy balls of fur with more loving pride than he ever showed for his own babies and announces happily, 'They're the best puppies we've ever had. They'll sell like hot cakes!'

Of course we often have a struggle to find good homes for them, especially as we are very particular about their future owners. In addition, Johnny has a weakness for 'sweet little bitches' and can't bring himself to part with them.

'She's the prettiest little bitch we've ever had,' he tells me. Or else, 'She's the cleverest one of the whole litter. It doesn't matter that she's ugly, the ugly ones often make the best dogs. She'll make a splendid sheep dog, I can always tell. We couldn't possible let her go.'

So we keep her, and in time she has sweet little bitches of her own and the cleverest little dogs Johnny has ever known. Thus, in spite of strenuous home-finding activities (mostly on my part), our doggy population has inexorably grown from our two Labradors to a permanent average of seven or eight, and we haven't fallen below four for years.

On one occasion two of our bitches had had litters at the same time and I had puppies all over the kitchen, under my feet all day.

I remarked to Johnny, 'We really must get a kennel made.'

'A kennel maid!' he replied. 'Have you gone completely round the bend? We have quite enough staff already with all your women. Who do you think you are – Lorna, Countess Howe?'

A sheep farmer or shepherd would be lost without his dog. Sheep range over large areas and often have to be gathered for some purpose or other. It is a mistake to imagine that all a sheep farmer has to do is turn them out to grass while he gets on with his ploughing or cultivation, or foregathers with his friends in the beer tent at point-to-points.

A good sheepdog from a well-known strain can cost more than £100. We know farmers who have paid £50 or £60 for their dogs, but the average Exmoor farmer is content with a dog he has either bred or trained himself, or has bought as a puppy for a few pounds. They are nonetheless invaluable and their masters prize them above rubies. Indeed I suspect that many a farmer's most important possessions, to his way of thinking, are his dog, his horse and his wife, in that order.

Shepherds have wonderful tales to tell about their dogs.

An old man came up to Nethercote one day on a coal lorry, just for the ride from Dulverton. He said it was 60 years since he had visited the farm as a boy. He inspected the buildings and told me of various features which had disappeared or been altered since his boyhood. Then he added that the tenant in those days had a dog called Forest. This tenant would gather his sheep on Bye Common, where in summer the tall bracken hid them from view, and drive them down to Nethercote. If, after counting them, he found that a few sheep had been left behind, he would send Forest back to find them, holding up the fingers of one hand to indicate how many were missing.

As long as the amount didn't exceed five, the dog would

invariably come back with the right number of sheep, even if it took him all day to locate and gather them.

Very occasionally, a sheepdog will take to killing sheep. When this happens, the only thing for his owner to do is to shoot him at once, unless he is lucky enough to have friends who live right away from sheep country and who will take the dog at a moment's notice.

Such a dog won't be vicious; on the contrary, he will probably be gentle and affectionate with human beings, making his master's grim task all the more difficult. It is often the most highly intelligent dogs who cross the thin dividing line between controlling the sheep and attacking them. They will lead a Jekyll and Hyde existence, working with the sheep perfectly during the day at their master's bidding and stealing off at dusk on the prowl for a victim.

Luckily such tragedies are rare, but they can be heartbreaking, as we know from personal experience. We once had two young Labradors, Twist and Honey, Leader's son and daughter. We had found a sheep dead, obviously killed by dogs, and were on the watch. Then Johnny caught Twist and Honey in the act of worrying another; they had it down on the ground and he was only just in time to save it.

We loved those two dogs but we knew there could be no weakening; both would have to be shot.

Johnny took his gun and told me to keep hold of Twist in case he tried to make off – for dogs have an unerring premonition. Then he led Honey away, beyond my sight. I stayed in the implement shed, holding Twist by a piece of string tied loosely round his neck. He was shivering. I stroked him, forcing myself to speak to him cheerfully, trying to pretend nothing was going to happen. He went on trembling from head to foot, while I stood there in the silence of the afternoon, waiting for the shot, with the string shaking between my fingers.

At last Johnny came back, white-faced.

'I've done Honey,' he said, 'I can't do it again. It's no good, I can't shoot Twist. You can let him go.'

'Thank God,' I thought, as I released him, and at once he stopped shivering and wagged his tail.

We both knew very clearly this was no solution to the problem. The only alternative was to keep him constantly tied up or shut in. That sort of life would be worse than death for him, and even if we imposed such perpetual restraint he would be bound, sooner or later, to break free. We would never have a moment's peace of mind. We shut him in the stable overnight, but my heart was heavy because I knew the inevitable was only postponed and would have to be faced.

The next morning, out of the blue, the postman brought us a letter from a stranger. The writer, who lived in Weybridge, in Surrey, said that he and his wife had been walking through our farm in the summer and had noticed we had some Labrador puppies. If we happened still to have one, would we sell it?

I wrote back at once to tell them that all our puppies were sold, as indeed they were, would they accept a two-year-old dog instead? I explained that he had been chasing sheep and needed (oh so badly needed) a home like theirs, far from any flock. I didn't dare tell them he had helped to kill one, for I was afraid this might put them off. But I was sure he would be all right with them.

They did have him. Some months later they sent us a photo of a tail-wagging Twist in their garden, surrounded by happy children. We could not have been more thankful.

A hound belonging to a visiting hunt wasn't so lucky, although it wasn't to blame. The hunt had been here for a week and were boxing the hounds to take them home when one escaped and couldn't be caught. The result was that it lived wild for some time, and having to find its own food started to kill sheep. It was a large white hound, their champion on whom they set great store for breeding purposes.

The police phoned us one morning to tell us it was in our area. It had killed some sheep at Simonsbath the previous day and they had tracked it that morning to Court Farm, at Exford. Someone had fired at it and missed and they had lost track of it, since when it had killed another sheep and was last seen making off towards Room Hill. They said they had 12 guns out after it and would we let them know at once if we sighted it.

Tom immediately went off on Sunshine to make sure our sheep were all right. Two had already been killed a few days earlier; we had found them with their throats torn out and partly eaten. The sheep were safe and Tom saw no sign of the hound, but the butcher saw it at Larcombe Foot that afternoon, when he was delivering meat to our box. It was next heard of in North Devon, where a West Regional News bulletin announced it had killed 15 sheep at Filleigh and warned people to look out for it. Soon after that it was shot.

If only the hunt had advertised the fact that it was missing earlier, the poor thing might have been found while it was still tame. It all seemed a tragic waste to onlookers like ourselves, who didn't know the full story. Perhaps they did advertise and we never heard about it.

CHAPTER 25

Bees and the Jeep

With the farm, we inherited several colonies of bees, rather to our dismay since we didn't know the first thing about bee-keeping. We were also presented with a special veil made of tulle, black in front as this is easier to see through, which drapes over a wide-brimmed hat to protect your face when you manipulate the bees. The previous owner, Mr Blake, gave us some elementary instructions, which we did our best to absorb, and promised to come to our aid if we were in difficulties.

Mr Blake was as good as his word and rode down to the rescue in response to my SOS when we had our first swarm. It had settled on a gatepost, a great brown lump like a rugby football, and had to be transferred into an empty hive. With him, he brought a goose wing and a gadget called a smoker, in which he burnt corrugated cardboard. The mere sight of these strange adjuncts filled me with panic.

Using the goose wing, he gently stroked the bees off the gatepost and into a box. Then, once they had quietened, he carefully laid the box on its side by the hive, arranged a clean white cloth between the two, and lit his smoker. It only took a few puffs to start them crawling up the cloth, a few at first, soon followed by the whole swarm in ever increasing numbers.

I watched the whole process in a state of suspended animation, bundled up in overalls and leather gloves, hat and veil. Bees buzzed around us and settled all over us and I made up my mind that I would never learn to cope with them. But there was no escape, for Johnny declared firmly that he had no time to waste and that they (as with the rabbits) would have to be my province.

Bees are rather drowsy when they have swarmed, and in general are easy to handle at such times, though if you are clumsy and disturb them too much they naturally become upset and resentful. In theory you should be well protected by your veil and long kid gloves with elastic round the forearm, but they have a way of finding a hole in the veil or a space between glove and sleeve, or between boot and trouser leg, up which they crawl.

The one thing to remember is not to panic. A bee won't sting if it can help it because it commits suicide by so doing, although it will sting if it thinks its queen is in danger. It takes some willpower not to flap when a bee is buzzing around your neck inside your veil, or wandering about inside your shirt. I once had so many flying around under my skirt and crawling up my legs that I had, as gently as possible, to slip out of my skirt in the middle of the orchard and stand there stock still in my flimsies while the bees made up their minds to leave me, one by one. But I wasn't stung.

After I had summoned our bee expert from across the valley on a couple of occasions, I hesitated to bother him again and decided to tackle the next swarm by myself. But they settled on a branch so high above my head I was unable to reach up and shake it and at the same time hold the box underneath to catch them. Poor Johnny always gets the worst of it, for I implore him to come and hold the box; while I stand there secure in my protective covering he has none and invariably gets stung in some particularly painful place – like the inside of the nostril. My bee-keeping activities aren't popular with him. I have now acquired a second bee-handling rig-out for him, since even after all these years I am usually unable to manage without his assistance.

Sometimes the bees will travel a long way when they are swarming, and if you don't spot them in the process, you can't find the swarm. If a swarm remains undetected it will generally stay where it has come down for some hours, most often overnight, taking off as soon as the morning sun comes round onto it. But first, scouts go out on reconnaissance to find new premises for the colony; these report back to the main forces and then guide them to their fresh quarters, perhaps in a hollow tree or up a chimney.

One morning Johnny was walking up Great Leys lane, the steep track which leads to the top of the farm, when he spied a swarm two-thirds of the way up, in a bush perched on top of the high grass bank on the right. The only way to reach it was to stand on the bonnet of the tractor. Disgruntled because he was busy, he went back to fetch the tractor and a box and cloth and with some difficult dislodged the swarm. He then placed the box under the bush on top of the bank, so the remaining bees would go in, and left them to settle.

An hour later, he set off up Great Leys again to collect the shooting brake, which he had left at the top of the farm. He took Tommie with him in the Jeep, giving her some sketchy instructions so she could drive it back for him.

Tommie had only had a little practice on the flat, so it was with her heart in her mouth that she started back down the steep lane. When she had crept about a third of the way, the steering suddenly failed. Johnny, who was following behind in the shooting brake, was horrified to see the Jeep swerve to the right, mount the bank at the side and overturn into the lane, trapping Tommie underneath.

Yanking on the handbrake, he jumped out and yelled to Tommie, 'Are you all right?'

'Yes,' came the muffled answer, hardly to be heard above the buzzing of thousands of agitated bees which filled the air.

At the same moment the shooting brake started to move on the steep slope and descended on the Jeep. Luckily it missed it, embedding itself in the bank, just above the box of bees.

Everything sorted itself out in due course and Tommie emerged unscathed from her ordeal and remarkably cheerful. After lunch, Johnny took the tractor up the lane and rigged up a pulley on it, with which he managed to right the Jeep. Then tractor, Jeep and shooting brake had to be driven home in turn, so very little farm work was done that day and it was late afternoon by the time he could think of the bees.

All our hives were full and we had no room for the new swarm, but Johnny knew a bee-keeper in Exford to whom he had promised any spare swarm we might have. He therefore walked up the lane again in the early evening and saw from afar, as he approached the box, that there were still a few bees circling round which hadn't yet joined their friends within. So he sat down a few yards away and smoked his pipe until they gradually disappeared inside. Then he crept up to the bank, reached up for the cloth which he had left there and whisked it over the top of the box to imprison the bees.

He made his way down the lane, holding the box as

gingerly as a newborn baby, placed it carefully in the back of the Jeep, and drove to Exford. There he found his friend, who took the box from him and was most grateful, promising to come over the next day and lend a hand with hay-making.

Johnny set off homewards, but hadn't gone far before he saw a cricket match in progress and stopped to watch. About ten minutes later the bee enthusiast arrived, with the shattering news that when he had removed the cloth there were only six bees in the box. There was general merriment and it took poor Johnny some time to live it down. Evidently the morning's earth tremors had been too much for the swarm and it had removed itself to safer shelter. We never found it. The disappointed bee-keeper arrived nevertheless to help with the hay.

The Jeep suffered no ill effects from its somersault and Johnny soon put the steering right.

I seemed to be dogged by bad luck almost every time I drove the Jeep and was always having to abandon it somewhere on the road between Minehead and Winsford with a broken fan belt or slipping clutch and hitch a lift, to be followed by the painful necessity of breaking the news to Johnny, who had to retrieve it.

The self-starter never worked and you had to park it on a slope or else crank it, but that was the least of my worries. The handbrake was useless, which made it awkward to start up again if you had to stop on an uphill stretch. This didn't bother Johnny as he can cover the foot brake with his heel while placing his toe on the accelerator without any trouble. The rest of us, with daintier feet, had to use a stick to push the accelerator while our foot was releasing the brake.

Then came the day when the foot brake failed as well and I drove into our yard with a flourish with my father beside me and ran smack into the side of the house. Johnny was too busy to see to the brakes and we drove the Jeep in this condition for some time, fortunately without attracting official notice.

On one occasion Johnny had taken the whole family to a point-to-point at Holnicote, near Porlock, and we were returning up the long steep road which climbs over the moor. There was an endless stream of cars in front and behind us and they kept on stopping. Each time this happened we ran back into the car behind us, or rather, we would have done so if one of the boys hadn't leapt over the side repeatedly with a large stone and slipped it under the back wheel, removing it as we started forward again and then sprinting after the Jeep to jump in.

When we reached the top of the hill Johnny decided to leave the main road and take a deserted narrow lane which ran steeply downhill through a farm called Oldworthy and would be blessedly free from traffic. We were careering merrily down this lane when to our horror we saw the owners of the farm driving up the hill to meet us. Since we couldn't stop, we naturally went on. Alarmed, they waved us back. Then all the Johnsons except our *pater familias* stood up in the open Jeep and shouted at the oncoming car with suitable gestures of impotence and despair. By this time we were nearly on top of them and I have never seen an astonished driver react with such lightning speed, slamming into reverse and shooting back down the hill in front of us. Soon after that Johnny fixed the foot brake.

While our vehicles may not always be reliable, Johnny is

the finest driver I have ever known; fast but dead safe, reacting instantly and correctly to any emergency. I would let him drive me over a six foot wide suspension bridge with no guard rails and a precipice below, with quiet confidence – well, perhaps with my eyes shut and in an absolute panic, to be honest, but if he said he could do it I would go with him.

The trouble starts when he has no means of knowing whether or not he can manage some particular feat of driving, but decides to have a bash at it. He never risks any neck but his own. He will drive a tractor down gradients which no-one else would attempt and has driven the Jeep practically up the side of a barn. He is also pathologically incapable of resisting a short cut or a road marked 'Unfit for motor traffic'.

The Jeep was involved in several other adventures of which I was usually the scapegoat, but it was Johnny who was one of the two protagonists in the most memorable incident of all.

He had driven up Room Hill and was proceeding across Road Hill, a rough stretch of adjoining moorland with a ditch traversing it at one point. He was cruising along, admiring the scenery and the beauty of the day, and quite forgot about the ditch. The next moment his front wheels were down in it and had embedded themselves in mud and bog. He revved up in reverse, but nothing happened except that his 14-odd stone made the front of the Jeep settle more securely.

Just then he saw walking towards him across the heather a friend, a gentleman of even more impressive proportions than his own, Matthew Waley-Cohen. The latter rose manfully to the emergency and pushed and heaved while Johnny sat in the Jeep with his foot on the accelerator. Still nothing happened, so they changed places, but when Mr

Waley-Cohen eased himself into the driving seat the Jeep promptly sank another six inches into the mire.

Next they decided to leave the Jeep in reverse, pull out the hand throttle to give it more revs, and both get out and push together. Their combined strength had the desired effect, and suddenly out shot the Jeep and disappeared like a streak over the horizon. Luckily its wheels were turned and it proceeded to go round backwards in circles at top speed.

Now ensued the rodeo. The two stalwarts crouched on the outside of the circle, ready to spring at the Jeep as it flashed past them, but they always jumped short of their target, swallow-diving into the empty air. At this point Mr Waley-Cohen had an inspiration and darted across to the inner side of the circling Jeep, thus reducing his radius. Johnny then witnessed the wonderful circus performance that followed and which filled him with admiration and awe. As the Jeep shot past him Mr Waley-Cohen dived head first into it, like a porpoise, and with legs waving in the air managed to stop it. It was a spectacular and heroic achievement.

CHAPTER 26

Departures

Life at Nethercote always seems to be a hectic rush. However efficiently I try to organise my day invariably something unexpected crops up to disrupt my plans.

Thus it came about, when the children were young, that although I always meant to prepare their outfits for the return to school at least a week beforehand, somehow the fateful day would creep up on me and nothing would be ready. I used to make an all out effort for the boys, whose trunks had to leave in advance for Sherborne, but as the girls at that time were fortnightly boarders at a convent in Minehead, which I could reach easily with forgotten items, their packing tended to be left until the last moment.

On one occasion, in the autumn of 1954, my plan of action for the girls' departure was as follows. Morning to be spent mending, cleaning and pressing clothes and packing suitcases; departure soon after lunch to allow for shopping in Minehead before arrival at school; long list of clothes and shoes to be bought and marked. Memo – take marking ink. Here is what actually happened.

10.00   I start sorting Gillian's clothes. Take down to kitchen
        bundle to be thawpitted and brushed. Discover gym

189

tunic has large tear in back and needs darning. Whiten her gym shoes and re-mark them. As I finish, one of the soles comes adrift. Jot down new pair on shopping list. Unable to find bedroom slippers.

Retrieve winter vests, which are in trunk with mothballs. They are now too small, so dig out Peter's old ones. All have to be marked 'Gillian', are damp and need airing. Put bundle of damp clothes in airing cupboard, brush off old pair of slippers, and search for rugs used for school as blankets.

Eventually locate them, protecting polished surface under ping-pong table on landing, just as all dogs start to bark. Car is seen out of window, drawing up. Unheralded arrival of married couple whom we never liked, on motoring holiday from London.

11.30 Coffee made for visitors, who are then supplied with gumboots and old raincoats and with Johnny's gun sent off to shoot rabbits.

11.45 Johnny asks me to give him a tow with the Jeep in order to get the Lancia started. I brace myself, but he is in exceptionally forgiving mood. We proceed up and down steep bit between deep litter and stream, with no result.

12.15 We are half-way to Larcombe Foot and I am still towing. Lancia starts.

12.30 Start sorting out Hilary's clothes. Gym tunic unwearable. Hilary says a navy blue skirt will do instead. I suggest an old one of mine, too tight for me but rather well cut (so I thought). She politely responds that it isn't really quite navy. I understand. Inscribe navy skirt on shopping list.

Find her winter overcoat, which looks all right to me except for a few stray dogs' hairs. She insists it must be lengthened. Hopeless search for green wool Sunday dress and she remembers she lent it for the school play. (She never liked it and I suspect more in this than meets the eye.)

1.00 Lunchtime. Visitors return from rabbit hunt looking hungry and depressed. They have used six of Johnny's best cartridges and are empty-handed. I suggest hotel for lunch and they depart.

1.45 Cases still empty. Search for Gillian's sandals under all beds, behind curtains, in boot-hole in porch and in cupboard under sink and finally discover them on top of Rayburn, drying and caked with mud.

4.00 *Mirabile dictu*! We're off!

We are proceeding along lane when Gillian spots one of Victor Stevens' sheep on its back the other side of the river. Impossible to cross. I reverse Jeep as far as bridge below Nethercote Cottage, nearly ramming railings. Hilary runs along meadow and gets clean shoes covered with mud. Sheep rescued.

4.50 Whirl into Minehead and ask what time shops close. Told mostly 5.00pm. Mad scramble ensues. Squeeze into Floyds Departmental Store and detain assistants, who already have outdoor coats on. Assistant of Ladies' Underwear hauled back by Manager just as she is making her escape by staff exit. Nobody at cash desk to give us change. Manager obliges and we are shown out through back way.

Ridlers not yet closed but putting up shutters. Fly there and leave girls to try on shoes while I gallop to

Smiths. Discover I have left shopping list at Floyds (no matter, now useless anyway) and Peter's squash racket (to be re-strung at sports shop) in Jeep.

Search for tea shop – all closed.

5.30 Find small cafe open. Order tea, unpack new shoes and mark with fountain pen as marking ink left at Nethercote. Wipe mud and dung from Hilary's shoes with handkerchief.

Unload luggage at Convent. Leave Peter's racket with Hilary and make mental note to phone Mother Superior for permission for her to take it to sports shop. Leave for home.

6.25 Bowling happily along main road when curious knocking noise develops in Jeep's innards.

6.30 Seems to be getting worse. Well-drilled by Johnny after various unfortunate occasions on which I have ignored curious knocking noises, I pull in at Dunster Garage. Only one man in charge and cars continually pulling up for petrol, but helpful proprietor examines engine at some length before discovering front wheel is loose. He tightens nuts, with difficulty.

8.00 Drive into yard, to be met by Johnny, anxiously waiting for Jeep. He has found a ewe on Room Hill on her back with an eye pecked out by crows and in a bad way, unable to stand. He has propped her up under a bush near a patch of whitish grass and needs to bring her down. Discover Gillian's school hat in bottom of Jeep.

We set off via Lyncombe to ask if they can inspect sheep on Room Hill while Johnny is away at Welsh sheep sales. Delayed in conversation.

9.00   Reach Room Hill in dark. Can't see gorse bush under which ewe is propped. Drive round in circles following hedges and trying to find patch of whitish grass.

9.30   Ewe located, once more on her back. Load her into Jeep and I hang on to her. Proceed down Room Hill. Very wet and slippery.

10.00 Reach home and put ewe in stable for night. Examine her eye and think we may be able to save it. Bathe it with boracic water.

Find tea things still on table. Clear table, feed dogs, see to fire – and so to bed.

There have been many epic Johnson departures. We never seem to achieve these without unforeseen crises developing. There was the time, in 1956, when Peter had to leave for an interview at Durham University and a taxi was to fetch him from home and take him to Dulverton station, half an hour's drive away. It had rained in torrents all night and by the morning of his departure the Exe had overflowed and our lane was so deep under water it was impossible for the taxi to get up.

It waited at Larcombe Foot while Johnny tried and failed to get through with the Jeep and then with one of the tractors. The minutes were ticking away and it was soon too late to catch the train at Dulverton, but there was still time to make the connection to the north by driving straight to Taunton.

At last Johnny succeeded in getting through the deepest part of the floods, below Nethercote Cottage, with the second tractor. Peter was taking with him a large suitcase, as he was going on from Durham to Bedfordshire to begin his National Service. He had to stand behind Johnny on the bar of the tractor, balancing his case on it. He was wearing rubber boots and holding his shoes in his hand because the water was over his ankles.

They were slowly forging their way along the flooded lane, with a gale blowing and the rain teeming down, when Johnny heard, above the roar of the tractor and the wind, a thin cry like the scream of a heron. Peter's suitcase had overbalanced, and in saving it from falling he had been forced to let go of his shoes, which were bobbing on the water some way back. They retrieved them and he emptied them out and insisted on wearing them. He would not face the Board of Examiners in gumboots and left them with Johnny.

The taxi just made the train at Taunton, but the poor boy had an uncomfortable 11 hour journey in wet feet. The floods subsided very rapidly as soon as he left, and half an hour later the road was passable again.

The next trip down the lane on the tractor was Johnny's. He had to go to London for a few days. As the car was being repaired, he decided to go by taxi to Dulverton and on by train to London. The taxi was ordered to pick him up at the end of the lane, because he said that Hilary could take him there on the tractor and bring back the deliveries from our box.

There was the usual flap over his preparations for the journey. He rejected as unsuitable every suitcase I offered him. I produced a brown Gladstone bag of my father's, which was condemned as heavy and cumbersome and the wrong shape to carry a suit, awkward to manage and not holding enough for its size. My 'Revelation' suitcase was spurned because he wouldn't be seen dead with luggage fastened with bits of string (the fasteners have been broken since the beginning of the war).

I volunteered to climb into the loft, though without much hope of finding anything which would meet with his approval since I well knew that his own cases were now reposing at Sherborne in the guise of school trunks. But I need hardly say that the loft ladder had been borrowed for farm work, so I was reprieved. In desperation Johnny plumped for the rejected Revelation and I miraculously found him a leather strap to put round it.

Time was getting short as he polished one of his shoes in the kitchen while I polished the other, but at last he was done. Then, in his new suit and looking quite the man about town, he climbed into the box at the back of the tractor and put the case down by his feet.

Hilary started up and drove out of the yard just as Ralph Slocombe, the relief postman, rode up to the house on his pony with the mail. There was a further brief delay while Johnny, perched in the box, glanced through the letters, and then they were off, with 15 minutes to make Larcombe Foot and the taxi and 37 minutes to train time.

They were well on their way, with Hilary driving very slowly because there had been a lot of rain and the puddles would have splashed Johnny's new suit, when she heard a bull-like bellow from behind her.

'My case! It's gone!'

The case had fallen off and was nowhere to be seen. Johnny had been happily looking about him and failed to notice when it took off.

He jumped out of the box so that Hilary could go back on her own, as she could drive more quickly without risk of splashing him. She left him, turned the tractor and went off in top gear at a dizzy speed, leaping over the bumps. She had just about got round the first bend when there was a crash behind her and there was the tractor box on the ground. One of the bolts holding it up had broken. She got off, found a bit of bailer twine and started trying to heave the box up into position so she could tie it up where the bolt had gone. While she was struggling unsuccessfully, round the corner from the direction of Nethercote trotted the postman, with his reins in one hand and the other clutching the missing case.

'Quick! called Hilary, 'Fly after my father with it,' and the last she saw of him was his galloping posterior disappearing down the lane, with the case bobbing up and down.

She finally got the tractor box hitched up and once more turned round, driving very slowly on account of the precarious position of the box. When she arrived at the end of the lane there was no sign of Johnny, the taxi or the case. So she returned to Nethercote, where we imagined him in his new suit galloping to the rendezvous on Ralph's pony. But it turned out later that he had caught his train without the need for any equestrian feats.

There was another occasion when Johnny had a car waiting for him at Larcombe Foot. As we again had no transport at home, he elected to ride down to the main road on my bicycle, Stanley's motorcycle having failed to start. He was late and I saw him vanish from sight pedalling furiously and looking like a trick-cycling elephant at a circus. It wasn't long before he noticed that the handlebars were gradually closing in towards him, until finally they fetched up against his chest. The frame couldn't take it and had folded up on him. He threw my bike in a ditch and did the last mile on foot in a cloudburst.

No member of the family is immune from the hazards which lie in wait for us when we venture out of the valley. Stanley once took his motorcycle into Barnstaple to have the brakes put right and found himself with insufficient money to pay for the repair. It was Barnstaple Fair week, so a simple solution occurred to him – he would have to win some. He paid sixpence at the first booth he saw, where you drew a number and pocketed the winnings if your number turned up. Sure enough, four shillings fell into his lap, which was no more than he had confidently expected, and he then had enough to pay the garage and buy himself a hot dog.

CHAPTER 27

Army Manoeuvres and Electricity

There was a transformation in the valley one summer, for the army and navy selected our territory for their combined manoeuvres. The army were supposed to be enemy occupation forces and the navy were the underground resistance groups, which were making forced marches at night and lying up during the day in places of concealment at farms friendly to the cause. Some months in advance a naval officer had reconnoitred the terrain and chosen Nethercote for one of the hide-outs.

The manoeuvres lasted about four days, during which time the naval contingents had to make their way from Devon to Dorset without being captured. The army forces were deployed along the routes the resistance men were expected to take and were patrolling all roads as far as they could with their comparatively limited forces, which they had to shift from one strategic point to the next as the hunt progressed across country. The army had no idea which 'safe houses' the navy would use, but were allowed to torture their captured prisoners to extract information.

Our naval informant told us that the torture would consist of making them stand for hours against a wall with their arms raised and other such uncomfortable indignities.

The navy, on the other hand, were in ignorance of the places the army would pick for their headquarters.

Thus it happened that the army took up its position at Comer's Cross, at the top of Room Hill. This overlooked our valley, which was crawling with escapees day and night, and we feared that at any moment a military search party would descend on us from above as the result of their scouts' intelligence reports of suspicious movements at Nethercote.

The whole thing was intensely convincing and we all entered into the spirit of the fray with realistic fervour. All the younger Johnsons were at home and poured over maps to help devise the safest escape routes along lonely lanes and through isolated farms. We had to shut the dogs in the most insulated place we could find in order to minimise the risk of their attracting unwelcome attention by their barking.

The navy men were split up into groups of three and we harboured 18 of them, as far as I can remember. Hilary got up at 4.00am to receive the first party and guide them to the hayloft and was kept happily occupied for the rest of the day. It had been a blustery wet night and the men arrived drenched, cold and weary. They had been sleeping rough in open country on the two preceding days. They brought their own rations and Hilary was kept busy brewing tea, producing piping hot stew, drying out wet socks and attending with elastoplast to blistered feet.

The men came into the middle kitchen in relays to warm themselves by the fire, but officially the house was out of bounds as a hiding place and they slept in the hayloft and in the straw in the Dutch barn, well concealed in hollows between the bales. One of them, who had to show himself in the open in order to reach the outside lavatory, was observed hobbling across the yard disguised in Arthur's old milking overall, carrying a pail and shouldering a pitchfork for good measure.

We kept a constant look-out for the enemy. There was an alert, once, when the umpire's Jeep was seen approaching and was mistaken for an army vehicle. It carried a special recognition flag, about which our sentry had not been told. The sentry was a young girl called Julie, whose family were staying at East Nethercote.

The suspicious Jeep stopped in East Nethercote yard and gave the password, 'Is there a man about the house?'

Julie hadn't been told about the password either. Convinced the enemy was upon us and that delaying tactics were vital, she replied, 'Yes, there is. Please wait and I'll fetch my father.'

This must have astonished the umpire, since the correct reply should have been, 'No, but there are some women.'

She ran into the house and told her parents they must hold up the driver as long as possible while she alerted us. She arrived at West Nethercote panting and gasping out her news and our household burst into feverish activity of camouflage and concealment.

We were left unmolested by the enemy, somewhat to our disappointment, for we would have enjoyed the crisis and gladly suffered torture for the sake of our protégés.

Evening drew on and it was time for our charges to steal out on their long march across country to their next rendezvous. They were a delightful bunch of fellows and we were sorry to see them go.

Three of the most footsore and exhausted lingered behind

and Hilary volunteered to conceal them in the back of the Jeep and take them along side roads and across the main Minehead-Exeter road, the chief danger point, before decanting them in a safe area. She covered them with straw and set off down our lane. It wasn't long before she came on Mrs Ridd, walking home to Winsford from Nethercote Cottage, where she had been working, and stopped to give her a lift.

As she climbed aboard, Hilary remarked jokingly, 'You'd better look out, there are three men in the back!'

Mrs Ridd glanced at the innocent looking straw and chuckled. She didn't believe a word of it and reached home without the slightest suspicion.

Hilary proceeded along the back roads until she came to the point where one of them led out into the main Exeter road. As she approached the junction her blood froze; an army patrolman was flagging her to a stop. She just had time to warn her human cargo in a whisper before pulling up, stunned by the prospect of imminent capture. The patrolman asked her if she had seen any strange characters on the roads, to which she could truthfully say no, and after promising him calmly to keep a look out and inform the next patrolman if she saw anything suspicious, she was allowed to proceed. She drove on and found that her knees were trembling. It was ridiculous but true, so realistic was the whole exercise we were all completely swept up in it.

Johnny went out later that night and helped to put some of the escapees on the right road. On his way back home he called in at the local, where he found the army Big Brass discussing the campaign over their beer, reviewing their plans and their information and hazarding guesses at the whereabouts of their quarry.

And so I come to the end of my story. Our lives have been transformed in recent years by the acquisition of a fridge, worked by calor gas, and the arrival of electricity in the form of a second-hand electric light plant. Although we no longer have to fiddle with filling oil lamps (except when we are unable to start the engine) we miss their warmth and their mellow glow. This modern innovation feels like an intrusion of civilisation, which has taken away for ever some of that indefinable atmosphere of history and unchanging survival which you feel so strongly at Nethercote.

In due course the batteries of our new acquisition failed. It was no longer possible to start it simply by switching on a few lights in the house; you had to cross the yard and circumnavigate the barn to reach the engine shed, come rain, hail or snow. Once there, you had to swing a heavy handle round and round.

This was too much of a strain for me. Nonetheless Johnny, like any self-respecting conjuror, needed his female helper to assist with the mystique. First of all, as he was about to start his swing, I had to squirt ether into a hole in the casing – just two little squirts. This was the abracadabra of the performance, the magic which was supposed to stimulate the engine into life. How, I never fathomed; it often appeared to anaesthetise it into a state of complete and irreversible coma.

Then I had to stand spread-eagled between the engine and the wall. In my right hand I held a piece of wood, which I was instructed to keep pressed against a knob on a panel on the wall, while with my left hand I had to push inwards a knob on the engine cowling at the precise moment when Johnny, whirling the starting handle, yelled 'NOW!'

At bedtime, the ritual was repeated in reverse. By the light of a failing torch you made your way across the yard again to the shed. Once there, you pulled or pushed (I forget which) a metal rod, at the same time taking care that (a) you didn't entangle your clothes or person with the spinning flywheel and (b) a metal pin did or did not (I forget which) drop into a hole over which it hung suspended. Then, when the roar had died away and the revolutions ceased, you retreated through the night and groped your way to bed by candlelight. This was normally the goodnight task of a loving wife.

Came the day when Johnny, after much activity with ladders and tremendous lengths of wire, greeted my return from a shopping expedition with a look of well-earned satisfaction.

'No longer,' said he proudly, 'will we have to go out in all weathers at night. I have fixed things so we can turn the engine off from the BATHROOM.'

Registering amazement and wifely admiration, I was escorted upstairs and told to look out of the window. A wire worthy of Bertram Mills Circus now emerged from under the barn roof, crossed the yard and entered the bathroom through a hole drilled in the side of the wooden window frame. On the end of the wire dangled a stirrup.

'All you have to do,' explained Johnny, 'is pull the stirrup and out goes the light! The wire runs through the barn to the engine in the shed. We'll try it out tonight.'

Well, night came. Johnny was in a good mood, looking forward to the performance, and decided to give me a treat. I was to be allowed to work the wizardry. This was indeed an honour. We were both in the bathroom; I had had my bath and was in my nightdress and he was in the bath.

I had expected to have to wait for the miracle until Johnny was dried and pyjama'd and ready for bed, but he said

203

magnanimously, 'You have a go. Take hold of the stirrup and pull. Now don't jerk, mind. Give a strong steady pull but don't tug. Just a strong steady pull.'

Nervously I grasped the stirrup. I pulled gingerly. Nothing happened. There was a certain amount of slack in the wire and I had to pull firmly enough to tauten it. I increased the strength and steadiness of my pull. The lights began to dim and the stirrup in my hand reached the end of its tether, but the lights remained faintly glowing and refused to go out. I flexed my biceps and knotted my triceps and, holding my breath, pulled with all my strength, at the same time being immensely careful not to jerk.

There was a sudden ear-splitting twang as the wire broke away from the stirrup and snaked back like a whiplash through the hole in the window frame. I was standing facing the window, with my back to Johnny, who was recumbent in the bath. My hand, suddenly released, shot upwards and backwards with the recoil; the stirrup flew out of my nerveless fingers and catapulted over my shoulder to hit Johnny smartly on his, laying him out under the water. I toppled backwards on top of him and simultaneously the dimmed lights brightened and blazed forth as they had never blazed before.

When we had sorted ourselves out and I was about to make a tentative apology, Johnny, ejecting a mouthful of soapy water, declared roundly and emphatically, 'You JERKED.' Before I could protest he went on, 'You gave a jerk and you've ruined everything and now, what's more, you'll have to go out to the shed and stop the engine.'

If he hadn't said I'd jerked, I believe I would have gone, in spite of the rain and my hot bath and now soaked nightdress. But the hideous injustice left me speechless. Though not so speechless that I couldn't tell him, as he lay pink and spluttering, with his shoulder turning gently purple, that I was off to bed and the lights could blaze all night for all I cared. And off to bed I swept. It was Johnny who braved the elements to turn the lights out.

Undeterred, the next day he fixed up his arrangement with wire and stirrup once more and it functioned without any further mishap until no longer needed. But the stirrup still hangs inside the bathroom window.

Postscript

My parents spent the rest of their lives at Nethercote. They expanded the farm, buying East Nethercote from Mrs Stevens (who moved with Victor to Larcombe Foot), and my brother Stanley later bought the cottage. My mother died in 1987, my father in 1992. I myself lived there for many years although I have now moved away, but Stanley and his daughter Rachel and their families still maintain a presence in the valley.

As my mother hoped, over the years Nethercote has remained a constant in the lives of her children, grandchildren and great-grandchildren, wherever we are. It is a place which, for those who have spent time there, becomes ingrained in our DNA. It may sometimes, as she experienced, be hard to live there; it is always hard to leave.

Birdie